Good Luck
&
Best Wishes
for your future plans
Sarala

Best Wishes for
the future -
Safe Journey
Chris
2

Hope all goes well
for you
Sorry you're leaving
love Maureen
x †

Best Wishes
Jayne

Best wishes
& good luck
sail with you,
you'll be missed
Love Brenda x

I'll be
off to
summer
the best
time
Take care, some sun
'n' have a
are here!
Marinood
x

Best of Luck
in your
New venture
Radha (crazy)!

Hope it's all plain
sailing to the
next port.
Good Luck &
Best wishes
Patricia

Good bye
Good luck
Bon Voyage.
Barbara W

It's been very nice
working with you.
Good Luck for the
future Wendy x

Sorry to see you go
Love
Barbara A. x

All good
wishes
for the future
Anne. H.C.A.

All the best
for a very
happy future
Tricia J.

All Good Wishes
& Good luck
Pat Dwyer. HV.

BT Global Challenge

Only
Wind
and *Water*

BT Global Challenge

Only
Wind
and *Water*

Author **Michael Calvin**   *Photographer* **Mark Pepper**
Foreword by **HRH *The Princess Royal***

PUBLISHED BY
SALAMANDER BOOKS LIMITED
LONDON

A Salamander Book

PUBLISHED BY SALAMANDER BOOKS LTD
129–137 YORK WAY
LONDON N7 9LG
UNITED KINGDOM

© (BOOK FORMAT) SALAMANDER BOOKS LTD 1997
© (ORIGINAL TEXT AND PICTURES) BRITISH TELECOMMUNICATIONS PLC 1997
PHME 29410/9/97

ISBN 0 86101 991 1

1 3 5 7 9 8 6 4 2

ALL CORRESPONDENCE CONCERNING THE CONTENT OF THIS VOLUME SHOULD BE
ADDRESSED TO SALAMANDER BOOKS LTD.

Credits

PROJECT EDITOR: CHRISTOPHER WESTHORP
DESIGNER: MARK HOLT
PICTURE RESEARCHER: ALI MCKICHAN
ENDPAPER MAP: © DAVID ATKINSON
YACHT CUTAWAY ARTWORK: © ERIC NORTH
TEXT FILM: SX DTP LTD, ENGLAND
COLOUR REPRODUCTION: EMIRATES PRINTING PRESS, UAE
PRINTED IN ITALY

PAGE 1: A WAVE ENGULFS THE HELM AREA.
PAGES 2–3: A BT GLOBAL CHALLENGE CREW STRUGGLES AGAINST THE TWIN
ELEMENTS OF WIND AND WATER.
PAGES 4–5: THE YACHT'S BOW SCYTHES THROUGH THE OCEAN.
PAGE 6: HRH THE PRINCESS ROYAL NAMING THE *SAVE THE CHILDREN* YACHT IN
ST KATHERINE'S DOCK.

Contents

Foreword

by HRH The Princess Royal

As Patron of the Challenge Races, it has been with keen interest that I have followed the yachts and their adventures around the world, in this second Global Challenge event.

The fourteen identical 67' yachts and crews set sail from Southampton on September 29th, 1996, and some ten months later the winning yacht, *Group 4*, passed the finish line into Southampton in the early hours of July 16th, 1997, successfully completing what will have been one of the longest and toughest sports events which take place.

Chay Blyth set out to create an opportunity for people from every walk of life to train and participate in a major yachting event. For the crew members that have sailed all the way around the world and those that have completed individual legs, this will have undoubtedly been an adventure of a lifetime and a test of absolute physical and mental stamina.

Sailing the world's oceans has brought the yachts face to face with the fiercest storms and gales blasting the fleet at up to 70 knots, lashed in freezing rains, on the alert for icebergs, to the complete extreme of tropical heat and the frustrations of the calms.

From all accounts sailing the Southern Ocean not only tested the yachts to their mechanical limits, but the tenacity and seamanship displayed from the crews which might once have been described as amateur, is a status which is certainly no longer apt. The competing teams have all risen to this challenge, and the celebrations and fireworks at the homecoming mark the completion of this incredible achievement.

From both experienced and inexperienced sailors there may be admiration and envy, but above all congratulations. Now is the time to reunite with family and friends, and reflect on the adventure. But for every crew taking part in the world's toughest yacht race, there really are no losers.

Anne

Press On

SIR CHAY BLYTH, CBE, BEM, does not belong to the Bufton Tufton tendency, the colourless worthies who habitually dominate the honours list. He may be a new knight of the realm, but in essence he remains the sergeant in the Parachute Regiment who decided that sailing around the world on his own was a cute career move. The fact that at the time he could neither sail, nor navigate, was incidental. He had enduring faith in his instinct for survival, and his flair for marketing the human spirit. The rest was hard work and window dressing. They called his solo circumnavigation, against prevailing winds and currents in 1971, "the impossible voyage". The description had a nice ring to it, which kept the PR people in clover and the headline writers in clichés, but it missed the fundamental point. Blyth's dictionary of life has no definition for the word impossible. He refuses to recognize the concept of ordinariness. His eyes, both literally and metaphorically, roam the horizon in a constant search for new challenges.

There is a revealing purity of purpose to the BT Global Challenge, the latest example of Blyth's belief in the common man, and woman. Like the inaugural Challenge race, staged, to huge popular acclaim, four years previously, it catered for those who prefer to do, but considered those who are content to dream. Ocean racing is a classless pursuit, and it was inevitable that the idea should attract a diverse range of characters, of all ages, abilities and attitudes.

The recruitment programme for the fourteen amateur crews, who sailed on identical sixty-seven-foot steel yachts, was unorthodox, and governed by Blyth's gut feelings. Little had changed since our first meeting in 1989, when I investigated the practicalities of fulfilling a schoolboy fantasy, and asked to sail around Cape Horn in the original Challenge race. I offered him column inches in the national press. He offered me a private showing of his favourite video, and, with a vulpine smile, left me alone in his boardroom.

Another world, as alien as the rock-strewn plains of Mars, flickered on to the screen. The sea was writhing violently, as if struggling to escape the suffocating grip of an unseen hand. The wind wailed like a professional mourner at the

LEFT: CHAY BLYTH'S *BRITISH STEEL* DURING HIS RECORD-BREAKING SOLO VOYAGE OF 1970–71.

LEFT: CHAY BLYTH'S *BRITISH STEEL* DURING HIS RECORD-BREAKING SOLO VOYAGE OF 1970–71.

ABOVE: CHAY BLYTH AND HIS STAFF AT THE CHALLENGE BUSINESS LTD.

graveside of an important client. The camera lens, splintered by spray, focussed on several insignificant specks, swathed in yellow wet weather gear. They turned out to be people, who had apparently lost all control of their legs, and were lurching ingloriously from one crisis to another.

This was a Southern Ocean storm, a thing of terrible beauty that tends to shut down the central nervous system. As I pondered its power, the door opened slowly. "Seen enough?" Blyth inquired. "Do you still want to do it?" With brain firmly in neutral, I answered in the affirmative. The rest, they say, is family history. Three years training and third place, on the yacht *Hofbrau Lager*, in the British Steel Challenge.

That race remains a pivotal personal experience, but some of the subtle lessons of the sea were revived only by the arrival, last December, of a familiar package, postmarked Plymouth. I had agreed to sail from Wellington to Sydney on the yacht *Motorola*, as part of the BBC documentary series covering the BT Global Challenge, and Chay's chaps had to get the paperwork in order. Embarassment was guaranteed, since the ordering of a new set of foulies required confirmation of my expanding waistline, and the formalities of personal insurance cover meant I sailed with the status of a war correspondent.

This was only to be expected. What was not so predictable was the vivid insight into Blyth's character, supplied by two motivational passages he sent to each crew volunteer. The first quoted German philosopher Johann Wolfgang von Goethe.

It was stirring stuff, climaxed by the entreaty: "Whatever you can do or dream, you can begin it. Boldness has genius, power and magic in it. Begin it now". The emotional double whammy was completed by the anonymous author of a piece entitled "Press On". It is worth quoting in full.

"Nothing in the world can take the place of persistence. Talent will not; nothing is more common than unsuccessful men with talent. Genius will not; unrewarded genius is almost a proverb. Education will not; the world is full of educated derelicts. Persistence and determination alone are omnipotent." It was enough to make even this cynical hack retreat to a long forgotten age of innocence. With a modicum of imagination, I could see the glint in Blyth's blue eyes, hear the soft Scottish accent caressing the words. It came as no surprise to learn he has the piece, encased in a wooden frame, hung behind his desk at his office in Menheniot, near Liskeard.

He has never hidden the commercial priorities of his projects, and his company, The Challenge Business Ltd, is diversifying into transatlantic rowing races, adventure holidays, and a series of corporate regattas on the Pacific Rim. The going rate for a berth on the BT Global Challenge was £18,750, a substantial sum, but acceptable value for anyone sufficiently receptive to absorb the particularly brutal form of self-analysis represented by a round the world race.

And it was a race, despite the sneers of those members of a dwindling minority, who portrayed the Challenge as little more than a strenuous activity holiday. The crews developed into an introspective community, with its dominant personalities and its dissidents. Not everything was sweetness and light, but the project had an essential honesty. Long-distance sailors are phlegmatic people, who can spot a poseur in an instant. The sea imposes hard truths. Anyone who ventures out on it cannot hide, from Mother Nature or their fellow man. It strips characters bare.

That, to be honest, is one of the principal attractions of such events to any student of human nature. Sociologists portray life on a long-distance yacht as being similar to being sequestered in a monastery, or serving a spell in prison. Certainly, being at sea for any length of time encourages an entirely new value system. There is a gradual, yet abiding, realization that what passes as normality is gauged by ephemeral matters, such as social status. The irony is that when you are never more isolated from what passes as the real world, you are never more attuned to it.

LEFT: THE FRAMEWORK OF THE YACHT COMES TOGETHER IN PLYMOUTH.

ABOVE RIGHT: WITH THE "SKIN" GOING ON THE YACHT STARTS TO COME TO LIFE.

RIGHT: AN ANNOTATED DIAGRAM SHOWING THE LAYOUT OF THE CHALLENGE CLASS BOATS.

SPECIFICATIONS

RIG: BERMUDAN CUTTER

LENGTH OVERALL: 67FT (20.42M)

LENGTH WATER LINE: 55FT (16.76M)

BEAM: 17FT 3IN (5.26M)

DRAUGHT: 9FT 6IN (2.85M)

DISPLACEMENT: 37 TONS AT HALF LOAD

BALLAST: 12 TONS

MAST: ATLANTIC SPARS

SAILS: HOOD SAILMAKERS LTD

WINCHES: HARKEN

DECK GEAR: ATLANTIC SPARS & LEWMAR

RIGGING SCREWS AND TERMINALS: STA-LOK

RUNNING RIGGING: LIROS DYNEEMA AND POLYESTER ROPES

ENGINE: 130HP PERKINS

GENERATOR: 27HP

FUEL: 385GAL (1,750L)

WATER: 242GAL (1,100L)

HULL CONSTRUCTION: 50B MILD STEEL

DECK: 316 STAINLESS STEEL

MAINSAIL: 974SQ FT (90.5SQ M)

GENOA: 1,480SQ FT (137.5SQ M)

NO.1 YANKEE: 1049SQ FT (97.4SQ M)

SPINNAKER: 3,780SQ FT (351SQ M)

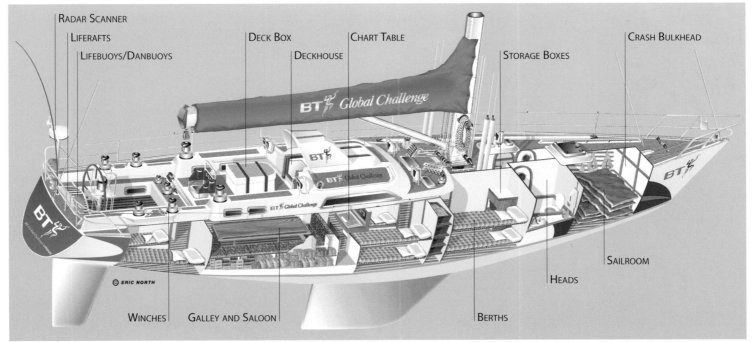

RADAR SCANNER

LIFERAFTS

LIFEBUOYS/DANBUOYS

DECK BOX

DECKHOUSE

CHART TABLE

STORAGE BOXES

CRASH BULKHEAD

© ERIC NORTH

WINCHES

GALLEY AND SALOON

BERTHS

HEADS

SAILROOM

Equally perversely, friendship goes hand in hand with emnity. It is impossible for a crew of fourteen strangers to gell completely. However inspirational the leadership provided by the professional skipper, certain characters mix like oil and water. The BT Global Challenge, for instance, highlighted the chasm in attitude between those who were obsessively competitive, and those for whom the event was a wider experience than a mere yacht race. The trick is to confront the issue of incompatability, but contain the emotional fall out. The collective spirit engendered by the sheer scale of the task should do the rest.

Some of the crew volunteers on the BT Global Challenge will fit back into jobs and family units with deceptive ease. Most will, sub-consciously, take several months to readjust. There is a haunting sense of freedom, which is double edged. It is rather like allowing battery farm chickens a brief romp in the summer sunlight, before herding them back into the dark timeless cell that acts as home. It begs the question of whether it is unfor-

givably cruel to offer an insight into an ideal, but ultimately unattainable, world, or charitable to offer a brief respite from a forbidding existence.

Everything is accelerated, yet somehow condensed into a finite timescale. Ten years living is packed into ten months, and the retrospective sense of enjoyment is overwhelming, despite the spells of utter boredom that can corrode initial enthusiasm. There are times, most notably in the Southern Ocean and the Doldrums, when every single fibre of your being hates what you are enduring. Yet from the comfort of a dockside bar, such trials and tribulations evolve into the days of your life. Being alive becomes a privilege, a thrill to be savoured and sustained.

It is sometimes difficult to put things into the correct context, to define the parameters of the achievement. It is sobering to consider that fewer than 300 people, out of a global population of five billion, have raced around the world the wrong way, East to West. No pun intended, but for rarity value,

that takes some beating. Climbing Everest, by comparison, is as conventional as a weekend visit to the supermarket, or taking a British Airways shuttle from London to Edinburgh.

The amateur sailors who left Southampton on 29 September 1996 were subtly different to those who returned on 16 and 17 July 1997. Nothing can buy the sense of self-esteem such a sustained examination of character can provide. The war stories, of huge seas, numbing spray, violent winds and strangely vulnerable icebergs, will acquire a theatrical edge, as the years ebb away. Yet these crews will still wake, in those reflective hours just before dawn, and mull over what they have experienced. Like Chay Blyth, they know what it is like to press on, regardless.

FAR LEFT: Seven of the Challenge yachts lined up at Devonport Royal Dockyard, Plymouth.

ABOVE: BT's training yacht sails under Tower Bridge in London during pre-race publicity events.

LEFT: *Nuclear Electric* about to enter the water for the first time alongside four other completed yachts.

Fab Four
Against the World

You know the feeling. You've agreed, in a weak or drunken moment, to a blind date. You turn up as arranged outside the Dog & Duck, with a pink carnation in your buttonhole and a rolled up copy of the *Pigeon Fanciers Gazette* under your arm to assist in identification. Given a choice, you'd prefer to be strolling naked through the lion enclosure at the nearest zoo. Your stomach is doing its best impression of a tumble-drier, your mouth seems to be coated with quick-setting concrete, and your eyes are frantically scanning the street for any inconveniently situated friends. Your mind, meanwhile, is full of politically incorrect visions of your date having all the grace and beauty of a tractor driver from Omsk. Help.

LEFT: THE YACHTS, EN ROUTE TO SOUTHAMPTON FROM ST KATHERINE'S DOCK, SAIL PAST GREENWICH, ONCE THE SITE OF A ROYAL PALACE AND A NAVAL COLLEGE, NOW HOME TO BRITAIN'S NATIONAL MARITIME MUSEUM, THE ROYAL OBSERVATORY, SIR FRANCIS CHICHESTER'S *GIPSY MOTH IV* AND THE PRESERVED CLIPPER *CUTTY SARK*.

This is, roughly, what Blyth's recruits for the BT Global Challenge were enduring as five o'clock approached on Saturday 6 January 1996. They were assembled at the London Boat Show, to discover the identity of the teammates with whom they would circumnavigate the globe. There was an awful sense of impotence and isolation, which the sensible majority chose to ease in the Guinness Bar. This is one of the great Boat Show rituals. The black stuff is such an effective anaesthetic that it is possible to pop in for a quick one on arrival, and to totter out into Earls Court Road some eight hours later, having seen not a single boat. I know. I was that sailor.

Happily for their livers, the crews were promptly ushered into an upstairs room, where Blyth theatrically outlined the teams, which had been balanced on the basis of age, ability, attitude and experience. Friends, whose relationships had developed during the initial training sessions in the Western Approaches, suddenly found themselves recast as rivals. Boat sponsors had chosen their batch of recruits, compiled after liaison with training skippers Andy Hindley and Mark Lodge, in a random ballot. With marketing campaigns to organize, and strategic commercial objectives to attain, they were as anxious as anyone to discover who would be first among supposed equals.

In such a one-design race, where the identical steel-hulled boats offer the promise of parity, a lot depended on the personalities and the principles of the fourteen professional skippers. They could be split into three distinct groups, The Fab Four, The Fun Boy Three, and The Munificent Seven. They were disparate characters, but all had reputations to build, careers to nurture. Victory in such a prominent race would be the perfect platform. Abject failure, in an event taken into millions of living rooms by the BBC's globally-distributed television documentary series, did not bear contemplation.

The Fab Four, Richard Tudor, Mike Golding, Adrian Donovan and Richard Merriweather, were skippers who had been retained after the British Steel Challenge. They had more to lose than anyone, and it was inevitable that their less celebrated colleagues should see them as principal targets. *Ocean Rover* skipper Paul Bennett, a former Royal Navy engineer fresh from the British Sailing Academy in Cowes, where he was senior instructor, admitted: "There is a fairly large hidden agenda. We're out to take a few scalps, crush a few egos, dent a few reputations."

Richard Tudor's reputation was reflected by the bookmakers, who installed his yacht, *Nuclear Electric*, as 2–1 favourites. He is an intense but likeable North Walian, who

LEFT: RACE PARTICIPANTS UNDERGOING THEIR EARLY SAIL TRAINING AT SALCOMBE.

RIGHT: LEARNING TO HANDLE THE BASICS ON A SMALL BOAT.

BELOW: DINGHY SAILING IS AN ESSENTIAL FOR TRAINEES.

inspired fierce loyalty in his former crew, on *British Steel II* in the previous Challenge race. They lost their chance of overall victory when they were dismasted in the Southern Ocean, and Tudor spoke passionately about his opportunity to complete "unfinished business".

Golding, a former fireman from Blue Watch at Langley in Berkshire, had similar sentiments. He had maintained his association with Group 4, whose boat he steered into second place in the British Steel Challenge. His project quickly developed an intriguing mixture of human warmth and cold, clinical precision. The warmth was supplied most conspicuously by Jorgen-Philip Sorensen, chairman of the global security company which sponsored the campaign. He is a vastly successful businessman, a feared autocrat, but is frequently reduced to tears by the exploits of the amateur sailors who wear his colours.

Sailing is an obsessively introspective sport, and many resented the extent of the support Sorensen offered. Logically, Golding, who had used the Group 4 Challenge yacht to beat Blyth's record for a "wrong way" solo circumnavigation in 1994, had little to prove, but the whispered derision generated by his unsuccessful Admiral's Cup campaign in 1995 irritated him. "To learn how to win you've got to learn from defeat" he reasoned. "Sure, I'm aware that some people are happy to see me fail. They just see me as some guy who has fallen on his feet. It's part of the game, and I won't change those attitudes until, in their eyes, I get out there and do it."

The regimentation of his approach mirrored the rigours of professionalism, and it soon became clear that the individualism of his crew members would be subjugated to collective ambition. As other crews headed back to the Guinness Bar, for a spot of liquid bonding after the announcement, Golding gave his team a pep talk about their responsibilities to themselves, the boat, and the sponsors. They changed into team clothing, and posed for photographs before being ushered away for the first of Sorensen's team dinners. In the months before the start, Golding put a key Admiral's Cup lesson into practice, and gave each crew member a strictly defined range of duties.

Donovan, on *Heath Insured II*, was a complete contrast. A laidback character with a wry sense of humour, he had survived the worst skipper's nightmare, the death of a crewman. It was monstrously unfair, given that he had sailed 120,000 miles in a professional career notable for several seamanship awards, but he was remembered, almost entirely, for being in charge when Bill Vincent inexplicably dived off the original *Heath Insured* yacht on the final leg of the British Steel Challenge, from Cape Town to Southampton.

Richard Merriweather's motivational qualities were enshrined by his galvanizing influence on the demoralized *Commercial Union* crew he inherited before the second leg of the initial Challenge race. As a blunt, no-nonsense character, who is not immune to the temptations of nicotine and alcohol, he was perfectly suited to crisis management. Patience is not

FAR LEFT, TOP: TRAINING SKIPPER MARK LODGE WHO SKIPPERED *MOTOROLA*.

FAR LEFT, BOTTOM: TRAINING SKIPPER ANDY HINDLEY WHO SKIPPERED *SAVE THE CHILDREN*.

LEFT: ACQUIRING A HEAD FOR HEIGHTS AS WELL AS A TASTE FOR THE OPEN SEAS.

his greatest virtue, yet he was aware he had to demonstrate his ability to build a new team without compromising his accustomed popularity.

Ironically enough, a race within a race soon developed with *Motorola* skipper Mark Lodge who, as Merriweather's mate on *Commercial Union* in the British Steel Challenge, was widely assumed to be his protégé. Lodge, together with fellow Fun Boy Three members Hindley and Simon Walker, was a star graduate of Blyth's University of Life. He was fitting suspended ceilings from a base in Canvey Island before the British Steel race. Now, after an impressive spell partnering Hindley on the fleet train-

ing programme for the BT Global Challenge, he had his own boat. He was, in every sense, a role model.

"The whole ethos of this event is 'go for it'" he reflected one sunny summer afternoon. "Well, I went for it. I sold my house and a couple of cars to get the money together to do the last race." He was visibly at ease with his authority, lounging back against the cockpit coaming as he oversaw the rigging work being completed by his crew. The air of easy humour which hung over the boat was accentuated by the scorn being poured on his haircut. It was the type of close crop that eases the pressure of a receding hairline, but is redolent of crombie

ABOVE: RAISING THE SAILS TAKES HARD, PHYSICAL GRAFT.

LEFT: A TYPICAL SEA SWELL DURING TRAINING IN THE WESTERN APPROACHES.

overcoats, button-down Ben Shermans and seventies' ska music.

"My crew know I appreciate what they are going through" he continued. "I can't mother them. They'll learn that anything you are subjected to for long enough becomes the norm, but they've got to take responsibility for themselves. They've got to get on with each other because once they get on this boat, there's no getting off. Like every skipper, I'm learning all the time, and the very fact I'm sitting here now is because of one very good human quality, the ability to forget. I've forgotten the scary bits, the horrible bits. They'll come soon enough."

The unsponsored yacht allocated to Hindley, my watch leader on *Hofbrau* in the previous race, eventually sailed with the livery of the Save the Children charity. Some people relished his initial discomfort at the lack of identity, and mistook his self-assurance for arrogance. Yet he had learned well from Pete Goss, our former skipper, who had recommended him as training co-ordinator to Blyth. He is an articulate, naturally talented sailor, whose attempt to create a vibrant atmosphere on his boat masked a deceptively thoughtful nature.

Walker, at twenty-eight the youngest skipper in the BT race, assumed command of *Toshiba Wave Warrior*. He also regarded Goss as a nautical father figure. His natural father Gerrard, a retired telecommunications engineer from Shropshire who enlisted as a crew member on *3Com*, had taken him sailing on the family thirty-footer from the age of three. "Simon wasn't like other children, who were content to play childish games on a boat" he remembered. "He wanted to handle the tiller, to be in control. It quickly became clear that he had a natural aptitude for sailing, and by the time he was ten I was quite happy to allow him to be in charge of adults as a watch leader.

"I'm not surprised he has been as successful as he has. In fact I think he can go right to the top of this sport. The world is his oyster. He has a natural authority, and can handle people from all walks of life quietly, but effectively. If he doesn't win this race, or come extremely close, I'll be extremely surprised." Importantly, his son's reputation was founded on something more substantial than paternal pride. He had proved, on the British Steel race, that he was one to be watched.

As mate, Walker was the pivotal figure on the yacht *Rhône-Poulenc*. He was a calming influence on a turbulent crew who were on their third skipper, Peter Phillips, before they left Rio de Janeiro at the start of the second leg to Hobart. He worked incessantly, understood the group dynamics of a complex set of characters, and had no compunction in demanding their confidence. Phillips, a Falstaffian figure hired as a troubleshooter, was content to give him his head, and increasingly relied upon his strength of will.

The Munificent Seven, products of Blyth's skipper recruitment programme, shared the earnest ambition of relative newcomers. They were given a four-day crash course in man-management in the spring, and were charged with putting theory into practice. Some, like Irish helicopter pilot Tom O'Connor, who took control of *Pause to Remember*, had relatively little blue water experience. Several others, like Bennett and Dave Tomkinson on *3Com*, were accomplished tutors, who used their instructional experience to invest the race with a more reflective approach.

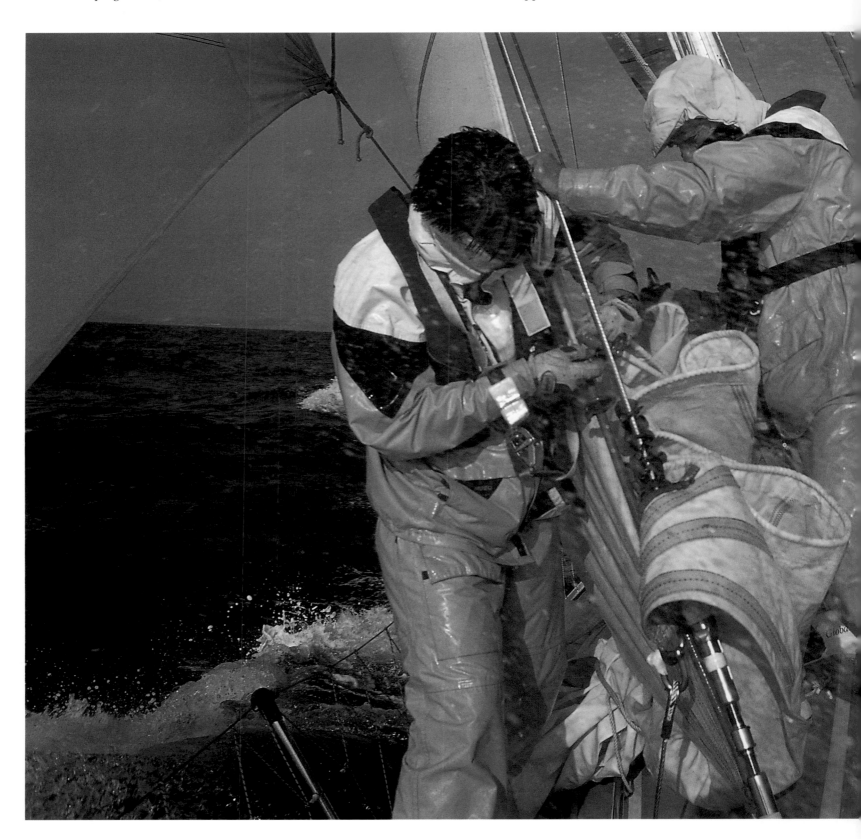

BELOW: WELCOME TO THE
FOREDECK CLUB. A PROPER TASTE
OF OCEAN CONDITIONS.

"One of the challenges is that if you actually looked at my crew they probably wouldn't choose to live even in the same county as each other" Bennett stressed. "They're different socially, financially, educationally, and politically, so it is quite a task to get them to live and work together, under pressure, in such a confined space. We have a set of values. Top of the list is no bitching. Human chemistry wins this race, because the boats are so similar. The only thing that is different is the people. If you've got a happy crew you'll be fast, but if you've got an unhappy crew you won't. That's simple psychology."

Bennett was one of several skippers to take a private pledge never to shout at his crew, even in the most stressful of situations. He preferred to admonish through eye contact, to analyse problems rather than emphasize them through personal confrontation. Boris Webber, the South African ocean racer chosen to lead the crew on *Courtaulds International*, encountered difficulties because of his voluble nature, which would pass without comment on the professional circuit.

It was all a matter of perspective. Webber, a straightfoward man with a long, soft face and the tousled locks of a rock musician, is, like us all, a child of his natural environment. That happens to be the cockpit of a racing yacht, which is no place for sensitive souls. Several of his crew volunteers on *Courtaulds* were discouraged by the harshness of his public criticism. Three were to drop out just before the start, when only Suse Goulder, Mike Leadbetter, Dave O'Ryan, Paul Collet and Webber himself survived from the crew unveiled at the Boat Show.

Chris Tibbs, another full-time racer, is less strident, but equally firm in his beliefs. He attempted to imbue his *Concert* crew with wisdom accumulated in his two previous circumnavigations, as first mate in the 1985–86 and 1989–90 Whitbread round the world races. He resolved to be a hard taskmaster, but in an understated, quietly spoken, manner. "A boat is a community" he explained. "The basic things in life become more important when you are out at sea, miles from anywhere, so it is important that, essentially, you like each other. In other round the world races, which rely more on technology, money is everything. Here we're getting down to basics. It's all about people. If it was easy it wouldn't be worth doing."

The sea does not breed showmen. It encourages humility, compatability and quiet application. Merfyn Owen, skipper of *Global Teamwork*, embodies the more cerebral approach. He is a yacht designer by trade, and since his first long-distance sail with the Ocean Youth club, on the infamous Fastnet race of 1979, he has diversified into campaign management. He ran two boats in the BOC single-handed round the world race of 1994–95, *Thursday's Child* and *Hunter's Child*, and applied for the BT Global Challenge after sailing around Cape Horn with Alan Wynne Thomas on the yacht *Cardiff Discovery*.

James Hatfield, skipper of *Time & Tide*, is more overt, more challenging. To him long-distance sailing is not merely an intellectual exercise. It is tangible proof of a man's spirit, an

insight into his soul. A thumbnail sketch of his background is all the explanation required. He was born with a hole in his heart, but his life changed irrevocably in September 1975, when, at the age of nineteen, he ruptured his aorta while out jogging. He underwent eight open heart operations over the following eighteen months and, on his own admission "started to lose the will to live". It was revived only by a yachting magazine, which contained a report outlining plans for the first mini-Transatlantic race. To a compulsively competitive character, imprisoned in a hospital bed, the sea suddenly became an overwhelmingly potent symbol of personal freedom.

He was, again to use his own words, "more dead than alive". He had no sailing experience, no yacht, no money, no navigational skills. To all intents and purposes, no hope. Yet, on the evening he read that article, he submitted an entry form. Within nine months, he was leaving Penzance in a home-made twenty-footer on the first of his twelve Atlantic crossings. He was named Yachtsman of the Year in 1987, when he became the first single-handed sailor to circumnavigate the globe, from the Pacific to the Atlantic via the Straits of Magellan. He raised £360,000 for heart research on the voyage, and was awarded the MBE.

He has a restless nature, a salesman's patter and the instincts of a streetwise politician. He saw skippering the first fully disabled crew to sail around the world as his destiny. yet Blyth, confronted with the idea, was sceptical. Hatfield, who viewed the BT Global Challenge as a crusade, was inured to rejection. He responded to the refusal by bombarding Blyth with evidence of his intent. He was never off the telephone, and, finally, when confronted by video evidence of the abilities of disabled sailors, Blyth gave his blessing. The subsequent *Time & Tide* campaign slogan, "Sailing the Latitudes to Change Attitudes", was not just an empty line of PRspeak. Blyth's change of mind might have been influenced by the inspirational nature of the ambition, but it was also a calculated gamble. He was reliant upon Hatfield finding a way to develop a cohesive crew from a collection of people given unique purpose by misfortune.

Hatfield's enthusiasm illuminated even the most dank days, when rain sluiced across the Ocean Village marina in Southampton. One afternoon, as the boats were being prepared for the inter-fleet Fastnet race in early July, we were standing on the pontoon as the heavens began to open. Others instinctively scurried for cover, but he refused to interrupt the tidal wave of words. He spoke urgently about the personal and collective significance of the campaign, using his arms to express himself when his eyes and his vocal chords failed to make the most of the feelings swirling around inside his animated frame. By the time he had finished we were both soaked to the skin. It did not seem to matter.

"Sailing has given me the world" he said. "It has transformed me from the person I was to the person I am. Heart surgery has made me a lot tougher on myself. I'm more demanding. I place greater value on what I get from my life. What is so rewarding about the Challenge is that I can look at my crew, and see those attitudes starting to sink in. To be honest, if I'd had to go through what some of them have gone through, my world would have fallen apart. They've left the 'why me, God?' syndrome behind them long ago. Life might have handed them a pretty raw deal, but they've come through the anger and the bitterness. They're after no one's sympathy vote. There's an urgency about them because they've been presented with an opportunity to be judged on equal terms. Most people look at the world and wonder why. My lot look at the world and ask why not?"

He made light of the responsibility – "people tell me it's awesome, but I don't see what they can't do. I see what they can do" – but the list of handicaps to which he had to adapt was

intimidating. The amputees on board had mobility problems. Communication was a central issue in dealing with deafness and blindness. Lack of physical strength was a problem for those coping with muscle-wasting disease, spinal deformity, or cancer. Hatfield felt obliged to be cruel to be kind. His best asset, almost his only advantage, was the indefinable spirit of defiance that made sense of his obsession.

Paul Burns had no inkling of how his life was to change at lunchtime on that fateful Saturday in January 1996, when he met up with Nigel Smith, a friend from the sailing section of the British Limbless Ex-Servicemen's Assocation, in the Guinness Bar at the Boat Show. "We had a couple of pints, and then decided to have a bimble around" he recalled. "It was just a day out." They wandered past the BT Global Challenge stand, where Stuart Boreham, a cerebral palsy sufferer who had become one of *Time & Tide*'s first recruits, noticed them walking with the exaggerated limp of amputees. Within an hour, the pair were on the yacht *Motorola*, outside the show, being interviewed by Blyth. By the time Burns returned to his home in Salisbury, he had some explaining to do. "When I got in my wife asked, casually, 'did you have a nice time?' 'Wonderful' I replied. 'By the way, I've just been offered a place on a round the world yacht race.' Her jaw just hit the ground and stayed there for a week."

Yet Burns had found a reason to believe. His motivation was all the more acute, all the more poignant, because of its tragic intensity. His left leg was blown off in the Warrenpoint Massacre in Northern Ireland in 1979. He is resigned to the imminent amputation of his severely burned right foot, which has been subjected to years of surgery. As one of only two survivors from the first of two massive IRA bombs, which killed eighteen of his colleagues in the Parachute Regiment, he feels a deep responsibility to reconcile the unnecessary guilt which accompanies survival.

"I was lucky really" he said, unwittingly flexing his one remaining leg, which dangled from his perch on the yacht's coachhouse roof. "I had lost my leg, had the other burned, but I was alive. I felt guilty. It was not just that eighteen guys had died that day. There were eighteen families, grieving, and I had got away with my injuries. That spurred me on, in a way, because the things I have done since I have not just done for myself. I've done them to bridge the gap, because the others were robbed of the chance to live their lives. They were the same age as me. We had gone through training together, joined the battalion together. We were in Berlin and Belfast together. Then, suddenly, they were gone. I think of that, and just feel privileged to be in this position."

The Fastnet race was a transitional event, and not only for Hatfield's crew. The five-day journey, an 850-mile round trip from Southampton to the fabled rock off the southwest corner of Ireland, was a rite of passage. Crews discovered the difference between perception of life on an ocean racer, and reality. They came to terms with the curse of sea-sickness and a whole

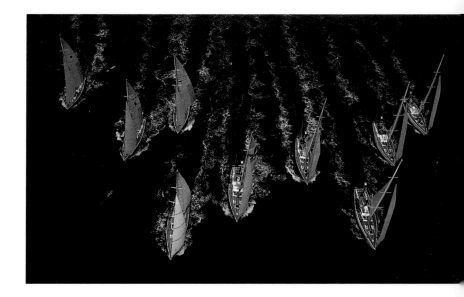

LEFT, TOP: THE START OF PROPER
RACING WITH THE BEGINNING OF
THE FASTNET.

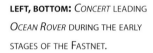

LEFT, TOP: THE START OF PROPER
RACING WITH THE BEGINNING OF
THE FASTNET.

LEFT, BOTTOM: *CONCERT* LEADING
OCEAN ROVER DURING THE EARLY
STAGES OF THE FASTNET.

RIGHT: ANDY PILKINGTON, SENT
UP THE MAST OF *HEATH INSURED II*,
SUSTAINED A HEAD INJURY THAT
ENDED HIS RACE ALMOST BEFORE IT
HAD BEGUN.

host of weaknesses that had been disguised by the phoney war of team-building seminars and private dinghy racing. Blyth stressed, in his pre-event briefing, that this was designated as a training exercise, but he might as well have saved his breath. It was time to make a point or two, and then sink a pint or two. Once the hangovers had cleared, a pecking order was established.

Tudor, on *Nuclear Electric*, led the fleet out past the Needles, and into heavy headseas. For the majority, a nightmare of nausea was about to begin. Typically, Jane Corfield was forced to retreat to her bunk on *3Com*, where she languished for three

days with only a plastic bag for company. "It was hideous" she remembered on her return, as she relished the sanctuary of dry land. "I felt so ill I could barely move to get to the loo. Next time out there, I'll have to wear diapers. Or take a suppository." Dignity, as you might gather, is an early casualty of life on the ocean wave.

More immediate medical assistance was required on *Heath Insured II* before the yacht had even left the Solent. Donovan was unable to raise the coastguard helicopter when mast man Andy Pilkington was hit on the head by the clew of the staysail, which pierced a blood vessel. The wound was too

deep to staunch, and he had no option but to divert to Cowes, where Pilkington was transferred to hospital in a waiting ambulance. The incident left them six hours adrift of the fleet, and condemned them to a sustained struggle, enlivened by a series of misfortunes.

Surfing on the gale-force winds provided an inestimable thrill, but the yacht's spreaders were bent when it suffered a knock-down on the way back from the Rock. Donovan then diverted to assist Hatfield, who was attempting to stabilize his boat to help a diabetic and needed additional antibiotics. Once he could do no more, he pulled out of the race. He preferred to make the most of the coincidental chance to escort Samantha Brewster, on the original *Heath Insured* yacht, back to Southampton at the end of her solo circumnavigation.

Tudor, meanwhile, was under pressure from Walker and Golding, who described the downwind spinnaker run from the Fastnet as "a demolition derby". *Group 4* shredded two spin-nakers, and Tudor destroyed one in a broach. Hatfield, in an early example of the meritocracy of the sea, followed suit. *Nuclear Electric*, however, held on to win by fifty-eight minutes from *Toshiba*. "It's an important win" Tudor reasoned. "The crew has been left with no false illusions about what lies ahead." Tony Mann concurred with his skipper. "Unreal" he reflected. "You're on forty-two tons of steel, with thirteen other

people, that is going up and down twenty, twenty-five feet. You're freezing cold. Wet. It's just like a rollercoaster ride at Blackpool that goes on for hours on end." Merriweather's crew radiated a similar sense of awe when they arrived little more than an hour later, just after midnight. "We've bonded" announced actor Sean Blowers, to the familiar hiss of pressur-ized beer cans being opened. Golding was fourth with Bennett, who finished just over a minute ahead of Lodge, the best placed newcomer in fifth.

Hindley had peeled away from the fleet when he was in a promising position. It was a diversion made by Royal appoint-ment. The Princess Royal was waiting to complete the formali-ties of naming his yacht at St Katherine's Dock in London. As patron of the race, she articulated its basic attractions. "It gives people the opportunity to do something almost unheard of in this day and age, to take physical risks" she said. "The very fact the crews volunteered from a background where they know lit-tle about sailing in any kind of boat means they are taking it on trust it can be done. What is so very encouraging is that sense of adventure and purpose still exists. I can only hazard a guess at what it must be like, hammering at the sea for long periods."

It was a time for hard, occasionally unpalatable, decisons. A dream is a nebulous thing, that can dissolve in an instant. Some of the initial recruits succumbed to sea-sickness,

LEFT: Richard Tudor and his victorious *Nuclear Electric* crew after winning the Fastnet – "An important win" he called it; the perfect preparation for what lay ahead.

RIGHT: Dusk in St Katherine's dock. The yachts wait for the big day while sponsors entertain guests.

BELOW: Actor Sean Blowers atop his yacht's rigging in St Katherine's Dock.

and withdrew from the Challenge, having earned the enduring respect of Blyth. "It takes considerable bravery to pull out at this late stage" he reflected. "But there is no loss of face because we know there is nothing worse than continued sea-sickness. No one should be forced to endure that trauma for weeks on end, and no one wants to end up as a burden to the rest of their crew." His tone was reassuringly emotional. Though the BT Global Challenge was his business, with an estimated turnover of £24 million, he ensured it never lost its human touch. "If it was not for the emotions it arouses I would not be doing it" Blyth insisted. "I've had my fun from sailing. I've had my time. Now it's for others to have a go. The whole thing is moving into a much more competitive phase, but there's still a bit of me on every boat, in every person. I love it. It's very, very exciting."

Other problems were quite literally closer to home. My brother David withdrew from the *Motorola* crew, because he could not bring himself to leave his infant son Jamie for months at a time. Peter, a second brother, who had developed into a key foredeck man for Tudor on *Nuclear Electric*, almost missed the start because of the birth of his first child. His partner Elaine was in labour in a Chelmsford hospital for two days before, at 5.30 on the evening of 28 September, Jack Peter Charles Calvin arrived in the world. His father spent three precious hours with him before he left to sail around that world.

The Long Goodbye

5,000 miles

Ocean Village is a soulless place at the best of times, a plastic palace of opportunism founded on the dubious merits of fast food and the quick buck. It did not look at its best when Peter Calvin arrived in the early hours of Sunday 29 September. A group of BT Global Challenge crew members, eking out last orders in the tapas bar, were all too eager to share his celebratory bottle of vodka, and his sense of wonder at the three polaroid photographs of his newly born son that would sustain him emotionally on a 5,000-mile journey to Rio de Janeiro. Heavy rain swept across the marina. An ever-strengthening wind played a discordant symphony on the denuded rigging of the fourteen identical yachts which were the star occupants of the complex.

LEFT: FIREWORKS LIGHT UP THE NIGHT SKY AS THE CROWD LOOKS ON WHILE THE CELEBRATIONS GET UNDERWAY TO MARK THE OPENING OF THE OCEAN VILLAGE AT SOUTHAMPTON AND THE BEGINNING OF THE BT GLOBAL CHALLENGE THE FOLLOWING DAY.

It was an eerie place, full of shadows, strangers and silent misgivings. A grey dawn did not improve the mood. Sleeplessness had been a common ailment in Southampton the previous night. Many of the amateur sailors due to leave, on a ten-month, 33,000-mile odyssey, were restless. They were in a properly made-up bed for the last time for more than a month, but were woken by the rain hammering on the windowpanes, and the realization that they had reached the point of no return. The unseasonal harshness of the weather reminded them of the consequences of a collective ambition that could only be fully rationalized in isolation. The most tender farewells that morning tended to be reserved for the privacy of hotel rooms; several wives could not bear the ordeal of saying good-bye to their loved one on the paved walkway in front of the gated door, attended by security guards, which led down to the pontoon. Those families who did part in such circumstances were distressed by the speed of departure, and its awful sim-plicity.

Fixed smiles signalled private pain. Anyone within a mile of that black gated door, which swung shut with a metallic finality that evoked images of a prison cell, needed a heart of granite. Fathers wrenched themselves away from sons, daugh-ters tore themselves free from the frantic embrace of their mothers. Many wept openly as they stowed the last of their belongings on the yachts. All Nick Auger could hear, as he clam-bered on to *Commercial Union*, was his four daughters, crying

FAR LEFT, TOP: ANDY HINDLEY
CARRIES OUT FINAL CHECKS ON THE
RIGGING OF *SAVE THE CHILFDREN*.

LEFT: START WEEK IN OCEAN
VILLAGE AND THE FIFTEEN CREWS
FOR THE FIRST LEG LINE UP FOR THE
CAMERA.

FAR LEFT, BOTTOM: TIME TO TAKE
PROVISIONS ON BOARD AND STORE
THEM FOR THE WEEKS AHEAD.

"Daddy, Daddy, Daddy". Tears, for souvenirs. Guilt, for a going-away present. Words were almost an irrelevance. I hugged Peter, as he stood at the foot of *Nuclear Electric*'s mast, attempting to gather himself. He was to tell me later: "I was completely spaced out". His eyes were red-rimmed and empty. His mind was on a hospital ward in Essex. "Don't worry, Mike" said a characteristically solicitous Richard Tudor. "Tell your folks I'll look after him."

Tracey Capstick, in the final stages of pregnancy, felt utterly alone. She poured out her frustrations in an article in *The Times*, which had sponsored her husband James, a mounted policeman who sailed away on *Ocean Rover*. "My husband hid at the far side of the yacht" she wrote. "I was not surprised. He was going, riddled with guilt at leaving two children, of ten and seven, and a wife who is eight months pregnant. We did not discuss it, but I knew it was there. Partners, parents, children and friends were tearful, frightened. Chay Blyth and I were feet apart, but might have been on separate planets. Over the past few weeks I have grown to despise him, and the round the world race that is his brainchild. As *Ocean Rover* disappeared out of sight, our brave faces disappeared, and we hugged each other sobbing, united in indescribable pain and grief. In the light of so much anguish, I was overcome with anger."

The wind was so strong it inverted the umbrellas shielding the relatives on the dockside. It gusted between thirty-five and forty knots, gale-force conditions. But the real power was

still applied by the imagination. As Jo Dawson, on *Toshiba*, reflected: "I am saying goodbye to everything I have ever known, to everything I have ever held dear." Hugh Fogerty, on *Ocean Rover*, was similarly philosophical. "The thought of losing a crew member really frightens me, but we are masters of our own destiny" he said. "People at home do not really know that. It's a lot harder for them." James Hatfield, amused at the irony of receiving a tax demand that weekend, made an unashamed lunge at the consciences of his disabled crew. "You will never meet the people whose lives you change because of this race" he told them.

There was no opportunity to brood. Once into Southampton Water the crews fell back into the rituals of pre-race training. Fenders were stowed, lines laid out, sails hoisted. The exertions were a wonderful release. Only the start, watched by a hardy spectator fleet of weekend sailors swathed in multi-coloured oilskins, remained. The Solent was opaque, flecked with white-crested waves. Cowes was cloaked with a grey mist and, as they circled the line at Gilkicker Point, the yachts hovered like hawks scanning summer hedgerows. No one wanted to make a mistake. Everyone wanted to make the first statement of intent. It was a perilously thin dividing line between

LEFT, TOP: THE RACE BEGINS UNDER GALE-FORCE CONDITIONS IN THE SOLENT.

LEFT, BOTTOM: AN EARLY ATTACK OF SEA-SICKNESS AS THE CHOPPY WATERS CLAIM ONE OF THE FIRST CASUALTIES AMONG MANY DURING THE FIRST DAY.

RIGHT: FLYING LESSONS. *SAVE THE CHILDREN'S* BOW LIFTS OUT OF THE WATER SOON AFTER THE START AND A CREW MEMBER IS SWEPT ACROSS THE FOREDECK.

those twin impostors, triumph and disaster. Only the start gun, fired by the Princess Royal at 12.05 precisely, mattered.

It had the impact of a death knell for the crew of *Global Teamwork*. Owen steered them across the line first, but he had jumped the line by ten seconds. The penalty, though seemingly out of all proportion to the crime, required him to put the boat into a 720° turn at the Needles, where he was ordered to wait for an hour in horribly disturbed seas, while the rest of the fleet disappeared over the horizon. Little wonder the skipper kept the punishment from his crew for as long as possible. Will Stephens, who as mainsheet trimmer had heard the race committee's verdict over the VHF, helped keep the secret. "It was a huge disappointment, of course" he said. "But I wouldn't have swapped the thrill of going over the line first for anything."

Had he realized the full extent of the misery which awaited in the English Channel, the temptation to make a day trip to the Isle of Wight might have been overpowering. Seasickness struck with a vengeance across the fleet. Watch systems were fragmented as more than half the sailors struggled with weakness and nausea. Typically, on *Group 4*, which had taken the lead from early pacesetters *Courtaulds International*, doctor Amanda Tristram developed a grim fascination with her discomfort. She estimated she vomited twenty times on her first night at sea. The boat's daily report to race control read: "Many seeing Saturday's dinner again. Everything seems to take twice as long as it should, with breaks to take air and visit the heads. Lots of groaning heard overnight, and bodies splayed on deck. Although not much chat, we were united in our thoughts. Have we really got 33,000 miles to go, and have we actually paid to do this?"

LEFT: *MOTOROLA*, *TOSHIBA WAVE WARRIOR* AND *OCEAN ROVER* ALL BEATING TO WINDWARD WITH THE VISIBILITY POOR. NOTE THAT *MOTOROLA*'S MAINSAIL IS REEFED TO REDUCE ITS SAIL AREA, AS ARE THOSE OF THE OTHER YACHTS.

Mike Golding's crew fell back, allowing Simon Walker, on *Toshiba*, to lead the fleet around Ushant off the west coast of France. Thankfully, the Bay of Biscay failed to live up to its fearsome reputation. Seas moderated, skies cleared, and a following wind allowed everyone to draw breath and assess damage. On *3Com* Kate Chaplin, an aromatherapist who sold treasured possessions, like her favourite teddy bear, to compete, persistently dislocated her shoulder. Hatfield had broken several small bones in his right hand, trapped between the wheel and the side of the boat when a wave swamped *Time & Tide* just off the Needles. He kept the injury to himself but, four days out of Southampton, caused momentary alarm by reporting to race HQ that Nigel Smith had broken his right leg. It turned out to be artificial.

Life on board began to acquire a semblance of normality. Mark Lodge, on *Motorola*, instituted a weekly showering roster, which allowed the ripest crew members five minutes of water and free use of the communal chamois leather. *Group 4* and *Toshiba*, first past the waypoint marked by the Berlenga lighthouse off the Portuguese coast, set the tactical agenda by pushing southwest. Others, led by Chris Tibbs on *Concert*, broke south, with the intention of hugging the African coast. This had been the most favourable route on the previous Challenge race, because of consistent sea breezes, but it was a gamble because the boats needed to sail more miles than those further out to sea. The jury was out until the Doldrums had been negotiated, the Equator had been crossed, and the southeast tradewinds had been entered.

Initial signs were encouraging. *Concert* took the lead, and *Ocean Rover*, another boat on the eastern fringe of the fleet, moved up to third. Tudor was following the same plan, which had won him the identical first leg of the British Steel race. However, his latent unease was reflected by a crew briefing in which he warned of the threat represented by pirates. Flares were issued, to be used as weapons against anyone who tried to board by force. They were not required, though the innocent interest of fishermen off the southern Moroccan coast, close to the Mauritanian border, created some concern. *Ocean Rover*, meanwhile, had a more tangible problem as they surged towards the Cape Verde Islands. The yacht was brought to a standstill, from eleven knots, by a collision with a twelve-foot shark, whose carcass floated to the surface just as skipper Paul Bennett and crewman Billy Thornton were about to dive over the transom to investigate rudder damage. With other sharks in the vicinity, stirred by blood in the water, repair work lost its urgency.

Temperatures rose inexorably, and the days hinged on the six-hourly position checks. The fleet was being monitored by satellites, orbiting 22,500 miles above the earth. Such was the uncanny accuracy of the system, the position of each yacht could be calculated to within 100 metres of open sea. This was an essential safety device, but also helped the race come alive for the landlocked audience. They were able to follow events through a fax polling system, the internet, or a multi-media package which took a year to develop. This link between the crews, their families and friends, was augmented by a high-

FAR LEFT: *3COM*'S CREW PUTTING A BRAVE FACE ON VERY TOUGH SEA CONDITIONS.

LEFT: THE CREW ON *GROUP 4* ALMOST OBLITERATED BY WAVES AND SPRAY.

frequency radio network, operated by BT Portishead. When Capstick became a father for the third time, on 15 October, it was his first point of contact. He spoke to Tracey, five hours after the birth, from the chart table. His first words – "Who's a clever girl then?" – sounded as if they had been uttered over a carphone on the M4.

His baby daughter, Georgia, had to live in his imagination until he reached Rio, where the private pressure showed as he struggled to contain his feelings. We sat together, on the concrete steps of the yacht club, as he pored over photographs of the child he had never seen. He is a proud man, whose voice broke with emotion as he discussed what he had missed. "I'm jealous" he admitted. "Lots of people have held my baby, and told me how beautiful she is. This is the first inkling I've had of what she looks like. Hearing about her birth was strange. At first it was just a computer message. I felt detached, isolated. Leaving had been very very hard. The last twenty-four hours were horrendous. People who know me will tell you I'm not particularly emotional, but my eyes were streaming. I wouldn't want to go through that again, but this is something I had to do. I came close to pulling out, but if I had done I would have spent the rest of my life regretting it. Of course it's selfish. It's got to be. It involves so much time, effort and expense. Everyone comes to terms with it in their own way. I think, I hope, I've got a strong relationship with my wife."

Tracey, meanwhile, was coping as best she could. She was not consumed by bitterness, as casual observers might have thought. She merely had the courage of her convictions, and refused to be part of a silent minority, condemned to watching and waiting. I visited her at her Surrey home, before flying out to Brazil. It was a pristine autumnal afternoon, fresh but bright. The sun highlighted the seasonal shades of red and burnished brown as she wheeled Georgia through a nearby wood. "When I came round from the anaesthetic in the recovery room at the hospital I felt really sorry for Jim" she said. "I thought 'Jim's really missing out here'. The race is something we've lived with for the past three years. These people have had to do this, for whatever reason, and I don't think there is any point whatsoever in not supporting them. You just have to live with it."

Defiant words, but they disguised real fear. Tracey, who was sitting on a fallen tree trunk as Georgia slept, had to stop speaking occasionally, to compose herself. "I don't normally do this" she said, apologizing unnecessarily. "It's just that logic tells me that a sixty-seven-foot craft is no way to travel the ocean. Though everyone tells me it is perfectly safe, and that all possible precautions have been taken, deep down I cannot accept that it is a sensible thing to do. We had one big row, three weeks before he went. That surprised me, because we do not normally argue. I analysed it, and eventually realized it was because I was frightened. I was frightened that something would happen to him."

ALL: A LIFE ON THE OCEAN WAVE. ALONGSIDE THE HARD WORK OF RACING TIME WAS ALSO FOUND TO RELAX, PERFORM THE RITUALS OF CROSSING THE EQUATOR AND DISCOVER THE WONDERS OF NATURE.

Such concerns dissipate over long distances. A round the world yacht race is a portable bubble, which protects its inhabitants from what passes as normality. Perversely, horizons are limited. Life revolves around the next position report. As the Doldrums began to envelop the fleet, these were a source of considerable disappointment to Boris Webber. His competitive instincts might have given *Courtaulds* an initial advantage, but, as the Equator loomed, they were in last place, eighty miles adrift of the nearest yacht, *Time & Tide*. They had destroyed their heavier spinnakers, and could not sail at the optimum angle. The protracted repair of their spinnaker pole, two feet shorter than intended after it had been hacksawed and glued back together, was another self-inflicted handicap. "The crew matured incredibly" he insisted. "There are a lot of stresses and strains that people ashore do not understand."

All fourteen skippers were beginning to realize the drawbacks of authority. Their weather-routing decisions were critical, and though the disappointment generated by flawed tactics remained largely unspoken, it was easily detectable. The antics of the crossing the line ceremonies on the Equator, where skippers dressed as King Neptune and administered a series of messy punishments for imaginary crimes committed by their crew, were a brief respite. *Concert* were furthest south, but had slipped to fifth place in an indication that Tibbs had taken the wrong option on the eastern flank of the fleet. Tudor was languishing even further behind, in a surprising eleventh. Golding's push west had paid off, and he led from Walker, on

Toshiba, and Richard Merriweather, on *Commercial Union*, which promptly sailed into a squall with a thirty-mile radius, and lost ground. "A horror show" he reflected. "We stood stock still for twelve hours, asking ourselves 'what are we doing here?'" Sean Blowers' sense of humour was hardly helped by gunwhaler's bottom, an irritating rash of itchy red spots caused by wearing shorts soaked in seawater. The only cure, exposing his backside to the sun, resulted in sunburn. Sitting down was not a pleasant experience.

At least there was a freshness to the wind as the boats surfed towards the Brazilian coast, in search of the warmer water that signals a favourable current. It proved to be one last trick of the elements, a final flaunting of the fickle nature of fate. *Group 4*'s advantage was whittled away within sight of Rio, as they were becalmed some twenty miles from the finish line. "It was an absolute nightmare" Golding reflected, as he indulged the luxury of motoring in to receive the Courtaulds Trophy, awarded to the winners of each leg. "It's one of the worst aspects of sailing. We were just sitting there, looking at the lights of the city, and worrying." Walker had taken a conscious decision before the race to monitor both the air and water temperatures in a search for fractional advantage. His research paid off. *Toshiba*, sailing along a breeze line, finished barely two hours behind, after making up more than forty miles overnight.

Watch leader Mark Earle praised Walker's "unbelieveable" tolerance. Like those around him, he found the journey offered a unique opportunity to people watch. "Everything is evolving" he said. "We're starting to gel, starting to give each other space. This is more, much more, than a yacht race around the world. We have to learn to understand other people but, at the same time, we're also discovering different aspects of our own character. It's quite surprising. You might think you are actually not performing that well, but someone will come up to you quietly and say 'that's brilliant'. It comes as quite a shock, but it's quite reassuring."

Tibbs, becalmed around Cape Frio, north of Rio, arrived in third place some nine hours later, in the early hours of the morning. It was a dispiriting time to dock. The yacht club was virtually deserted. In keeping with the prevailing mood, he described the final two days as "the most frustrating forty-eight hours I've spent at sea." Hindley, who steered *Save the Children* through the shadow of the Sugar Loaf as dawn broke, was happier with fourth. He was forced to sail conservatively after damaging sails in a spectacular broach, which he estimated had cost him 100 miles. *Commercial Union*, who were hugging the coast, appeared on the horizon behind them before they ran into a fishing net. The boat stopped dead from eight knots and, with the line weaving an intricate web around the rudder and keel, there was no option but to launch a dinghy. "It was daft" said a disenchanted Merriweather. "Like something out of 'The Last of the Summer Wine'."

Insult was piled on indignity when they were becalmed in the polluted waters of Rio's Guanabara Bay, which, like the muggers of Copacabana beach, deserve a place in the city's alternative tourist guide. The wake of motorized support boats was a putrid bottle green, and it was no surprise when one craft chanced upon the bloated corpse of a local man. Merriweather, who had the look of a man with murderous intent, decided music was required to soothe his troubled soul. Mistake. Blowers bounded below deck. Status Quo boomed out over the speakers. In an instant Blowers and David Shanks were on the

coachhouse roof, wearing red fright wigs and wielding a blow-up guitar and saxophone, which had been purchased in a Southampton joke shop. The surreal sight of them miming to "Rocking All Over the World" will live in the memory long after Quo get their OAP bus passes, which, by my reckoning, is at the turn of the century.

"The highs and lows come on a daily basis" Blowers said as Merriweather, by now resplendent in a silver wig which gave him an uncanny resemblance to the drummer in the Glitter Band, coaxed the boat over the finishing line. "On the one hand you have the natural experiences, the sunsets and the starry skies. They're wonderful things, at which you just stand and stare. On the other hand you have this, the most frustrating thing I have ever been through. I know we're fifth, not that far behind the leaders in what is going to be a long race, but we've just been pootling in. It has seemed as if Rio would never come."

The sentiments were shared down the fleet. *3Com* arrived as darkness fell, prompting their sponsors to release a blizzard of blue and white balloons. They were followed by *Motorola*, which had been sailed conservatively by Lodge as he detected his team's strengths and weaknesses. The most urgent race was staged in the middle of the night, between *Ocean Rover* and *Heath Insured II*. They had been within sight of each

other for 2,100 miles, and Paul Bennett, on *Rover*, had a fifty-yard lead when he rounded the final fairway buoy, a mile from the finish. Then he made the fundamental mistake of opting to go further inshore. His yacht, trapped in the swell, was unable to make any headway, and was almost washed up on to the football pitches on Copacabana beach. Adrian Donovan, helm-

ing *Heath*, made the right choice, and eased his boat back out to sea. It ghosted over the line in the four-knot breeze, nearly two hours ahead of a chastened Bennett. "That was probably the worst twenty-four hours of my life" he said. "He went one way and we went the other, to have a look at the beach babes. The only weak link in the chain was me."

ABOVE: A JUBILANT MIKE GOLDING AND HIS CREW WITH SUGAR LOAF AS THE BACKDROP.

ABOVE LEFT: *COMMERCIAL UNION* ROCKING TO THE SOUND OF STATUS QUO AS THEY ARRIVE FIFTH.

LEFT: DAVID HODDER OF *TIME & TIDE* IN REFLECTIVE MOOD IN RIO. A VICTIM OF SUSTAINED SEA-SICKNESS, HE DECIDED TO RETIRE.

RIGHT: CHAMPAGNE AND A CHANCE TO CATCH UP AS THE *TOSHIBA* CREW RECEIVE THEIR POST.

Tudor, who berthed two hours later, was not noticeably happier. "We're late" he announced. "Ten places late." The strain of favouritism was etched on his sun-reddened face. He wore only one deck shoe – the other was lost overboard – and a look of utter despair. Once his dejection had been digested, attention, in the following forty-eight hours, switched to the progress of *Time & Tide*. It had been a difficult month for Hatfield. The boat was being sailed efficiently enough, but sail changes were taking too long. Paul Burns suffered horribly from sores on the stump of his severed leg, and David Hodder required injections to survive sustained sea-sickness, which manifested itself in a series of cold sweats. The skipper's mood swings were accelerated by personality clashes with Stuart Boreham, the cerebral palsy victim, and Richard Horton-Fawkes, the glaucoma sufferer who was on the verge of complete blindness.

Hatfield desperately wanted to avoid the stigma of finishing last, but *Courtaulds*, the penultimate boat to arrive, beat

them by two and a half hours. Hodder had requested a private word at sunset some days before, and confided he was withdrawing from the race. "It's sad" the skipper acknowledged. "But David has probably made the right decision for himself." Hodder, who had signed up on the scant evidence of his enjoyment of a day's corporate sailing in the Solent, was visibly moved by the rituals of farewell. "I don't feel it's fair on the others" he said. "I work on the foredeck. It's a dangerous place. It's wet, cold. There's water up to your waist, and I just don't feel fit enough to contribute. I wouldn't want to be responsible if something went wrong. I don't want to be left saying 'I should have been there, I should have been stronger'. This is a great group of people, and I will be a member of this *Time & Tide* crew for the rest of my life. I feel like a world beater, really."

Regrettably, Horton-Fawkes left the crew with less grace. His attempt to have Hatfield replaced was unanimously rejected by the crew, who were gathered together by Blyth at the Rio yacht club. The skipper did not deserve the slur, which everyone else chose to ignore. The fleet saw through the petty politics, and the bickering that is inevitably exacerbated by life at close quarters. They saw only a committed man, a sailor of skill and substance. They had the BT Global Challenge in its true perspective. Just like Peter Calvin and James Capstick, who headed for Rio's Galeão International Airport, and England, to briefly reacquaint themselves with the realities of family life.

Questions
and Answers

6,600 miles

The questions had the predictability of a public bar drunk. "What's it like then?" "Are you scared? Are you cold? Are you tired? Are you hungry?" Those of us who had sailed into the Southern Ocean from Rio four years previously became used to an exaggerated respect.
It was flattering nonsense, of course, but the BT Global Challenge crews understood instinctively that there was no substitute for experience. They seemed in a reflective, almost rebellious mood. The socially conscious members of the Iate Clube do Rio de Janeiro kept their distance. They patently failed to understand the mentality of their guests. The only thing locals sought to prove on the sea was their wealth.

LEFT: *CONCERT* SAILING INTO WELLINGTON HARBOUR, NEW ZEALAND, WITH ITS BROKEN MAST IN URGENT NEED OF REPLACEMENT PRIOR TO THE NEXT LEG. THE TEAM MOTORED FROM THEIR EMERGENCY REFUELLING BASE IN THE CHATHAM ISLANDS WHERE THEY SPENT NEW YEAR'S EVE WITH FRIENDS AND FAMILY WHO FLEW IN FROM NEW ZEALAND.

The crews, preparing for what they believed would be the axial personal experience of the race, could not get enough of the war stories. My favourite, involving *Hofbrau*'s first Southern Ocean storm, was duly trotted out on request. It was the ultimate introduction to one's own insignificance. I was hunched in the cockpit, in the guise of winch monkey, as winds built to seventy-four knots. Down below, the force of a forty-two-ton yacht falling from plateaued waves was such that light bulbs were exploding from their sockets. The galley table was prised out of the floor. The deck was regularly swept clean by six-foot walls of green water, which gurgled malevolently. It was being deposited on us from the steeply banked seas that characterize the continental shelf just off Cape Horn. Fate decreed where you landed, but it was usually at the full extent of your lifeline. On one occasion, picking myself up from the base of the wheel, I gazed up at the maniacal smile of skipper Pete Goss. "Don't worry" he yelled against the hiss of a receding wave, "It's only wind and water".

Quite. Whenever the privations reached the point of absurdity, we would repeat that mantra. Chay Blyth – the knighthood was still a product of his fertile imagination at this stage of the race – understood. He, after all, spent nineteen hours in the water off Cape Horn, when his trimaran *Beefeater II*

capsized in what he called "the worst seas I have ever seen in my life". As he wrote in the *Daily Telegraph*: "Survive something like that, and you begin to understand the true meaning of your mortality. I've been advising the BT Global Challenge crews to expect a culture shock beyond their imagination. Their task has a psychological dimension, as well as a physical one. They've all been asking 'what's it really like?' Well, not to put too fine a point on it, the experience can be described in a single word. Horrific."

Richard Tudor also knew that essential truth. He was scarred, mentally, by the experience of being in charge of *British Steel II* when her rig disappeared over the side. I was on radio duty on *Hofbrau* that day, and he refused our offer of assistance graciously, gratefully. He spoke slowly, clearly. He was coping. It was only later, when there was too much time to think, that the magnitude of his disappointment would sink in. He retains revealingly vivid memories of the incident. "We rounded Cape Horn on December 1" he said, as *Nuclear Electric* bobbed on her mooring just before the restart. "Sixteen days later, we lost our mast deep in the Southern Ocean." There was a wistful look in his eyes. His voice had a compelling urgency. It was like listening to Dylan Thomas read poetry. "I shall never forget that day" he continued. "It was blowing forty knots. It

FAR LEFT: *HEATH INSURED II* PARTLY OBSCURED BY THE OCEAN SWELL OFF THE RIO COASTLINE AT THE START OF LEG TWO. ONLY THE SAILS OF *COMMERCIAL UNION* PEEP OVER THE WAVE.

LEFT: THREE YACHTS COMPETE FOR POSITION – *COMMERCIAL UNION*, *TOSHIBA WAVE WARRIOR* AND *CONCERT* – DURING THE MURKY WEATHER PREVAILING AT THE BEGINNING OF THE LEG.

was just before dawn and we had seen an iceberg on the radar screen, just over the horizon. It was pretty horrific. I don't want that to happen again, to any of these yachts."

To investigate the impact of the imagination, I chose to consider a single crew. Richard Merriweather had, on *Commercial Union*, developed a brutal honesty about what awaited. "I've told them for umpteen months that they're going to be colder, for longer, than they've ever imagined" he said. "I still don't really know if they believe me. We'll have to keep the ban-

ter up, play a few silly games. Failing that, I'll have to lie to keep morale up." He never needed to go to that extreme, because he had the complete respect of a lively group, who had no interest in empty bravado. "I'm very apprehensive" admitted Nick Auger. "The Southern Ocean is one of those things" reflected Tim Burrows. "We dread it. We all expect it to be awful, so it will probably turn out to be considerably less nasty than we fear." Lars Hultgren, the self-proclaimed "token Swede on board", said "Being a bowman, it feels a bit scary". David Shanks,

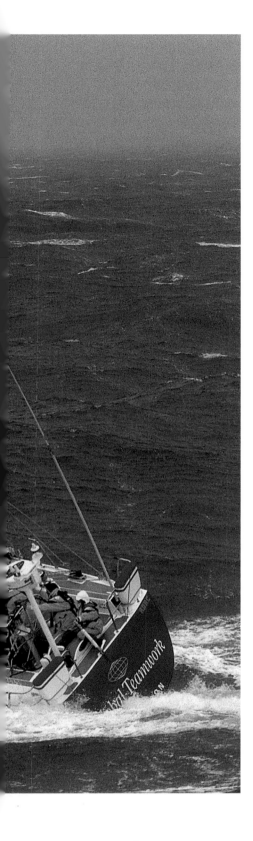

ABOVE: ALL HANDS ON DECK AS A REEFED-DOWN *GLOBAL TEAMWORK* CREW WORK THE BOAT HARD.

ABOVE: HUMAN BALLAST. MEMBERS OF *3COM*'S CREW SIT ON THE WINDWARD RAIL.

another coming to terms with the prospect of being exposed on the foredeck, added: "The thing about the Southern Ocean is you can't train for it. It doesn't exist anywhere else." Bransom Bean, who sailed nuclear submarines in the United States Navy, suggested "I'm fairly intimidated by what lies ahead. It's going to be pretty rough and that bothers me". Only Trevor Corner took a slightly tangential view. "Someone asked me why I am going around the world on a boat" he said. "Well, my simple answer is that it is better than going around the world on a bus".

There's no answer to that. But the ready smiles disguised the fact that Rio had been unkind to the crews. They felt isolated, unwanted, at the yacht club. The sudden death of popular sailmaker Peter Vroon, who contracted meningitis, shook everyone to the core. The local lowlife were a constant irritation. James Hatfield rashly threw a punch at one assailant and Tom O'Connor was mugged by a group of transvestites as he took a night-time stroll along Copacabana beach. His crew, unfulfilled by their twelfth place in the first leg, recognized their wider responsibility, to lead the fleet's Two Minute Silence at 11am on 11 November. Their sponsors, the British Legion, relished the platform offered by the BT Global Challenge, which they believed offered an "unprecedented opportunity" to unite ex-servicemen around the world.

The final days in dock dragged. A succession of thermal mugs, baby mattresses, and hot waterbottles were ferried out to the boats. *Concert* crew members were given two pairs of specially developed underpants, designed in the USA to keep moisture out of a sailor's nether regions. You didn't need to be Einstein to work out that, since each pair would need to be worn for a month on the 7,200-mile journey to Wellington, cabins were likely to require fumigation by the New Zealand Customs Service. Appropriately enough, start day, 20 November, was dank and depressing. Low cloud shrouded the beachfront high-rises along Copacabana, and obscured the statue of Christ the Redeemer. Fine rain fell with fluctuating intensity.

There was minimal wind, and Mike Golding's ruse, of attempting to drift inshore, did not pay off. It was left to Chris Tibbs, on *Concert*, to lead the fleet out to open sea, past the Redonda and Rasa islands. They were followed closely by Simon Walker's *Toshiba*, and Merriweather, on *Commercial Union*. The sponsors' fireworks, released by Courtaulds, did little to alleviate the mood. Golding spoke for everyone when he informed race HQ that "emotions are in turmoil". Hatfield, who in a fashionable gesture took on extra supplies of underpants just before the start gun, made his move on the second night out. No one bothered to cover *Time & Tide* when he veered back towards the Brazilian coast and, suddenly, his disabled crew were in the lead. He considered it a defining moment of the race. "They all thought 'oh we don't need to worry, it's only the raspberry ripples'" he said. "Leading was just the best feeling. It was everything that we had worked for."

Normal service was resumed within forty-eight hours, however. Golding picked up his familiar role as pacemaker, and the fleet received several wake-up calls from reality. *Nuclear Electric*'s Jos Walters crushed a finger as she struggled to drop a spinnaker in a squall – "I looked down at a pool of blood and thought 'hey, that's mine'" – and Andy Hindley was forced to evacuate Austrian crew member Kurt Kinast from *Save the Children* to HMS *Lancaster*, a Royal Navy Type 23 Frigate on patrol off the coast of Uruguay. He was suffering from kidney problems, and treated in hospital in Montevideo. "It was weird,

FAR LEFT, TOP: NICK AUGER ON *COMMERCIAL UNION* WHO HAD TALKED OF HIS APPREHENSIVENESS AT THE PROSPECT OF THE OCEAN FACING THEM.

FAR LEFT, BOTTOM: SAILMAKER PETER VROON WHOSE TRAGIC DEATH IN RIO, FROM MENINGITIS, DEEPLY AFFECTED ALL.

LEFT: RHIAN JENKINS AIR-LIFTED OFF *GLOBAL TEAMWORK* TO BE TREATED IN THE FALKLANDS FOR A SUSPECTED DUODENAL ULCER.

BELOW: RHIAN JENKINS WHO STAGED A FULL RECOVERY FROM WHAT TURNED OUT TO BE FOOD POISONING RATHER THAN AN ULCER AND MANAGED TO REJOIN AT WELLINGTON.

scary" said Hindley. "One minute Kurt was there, sitting with us. The next he was gone. This really big grey ship came over the horizon, did a handbrake turn to the right, and sent a rib, which took him without so much as a by your leave. There wasn't even enough time to say a proper good-bye."

The *Global Teamwork* crew were similarly stunned. Rhian Jenkins, suffering from a suspected duodenal ulcer that was eventually diagnosed as food poisoning, was airlifted to the Falklands by an RAF Sea King helicopter. As she looked down from a small porthole window, at the crewmates waving good-bye, her dream seemed to have dissipated. "I was just sitting there in a sort of daze" she said. "I felt absolutely devastated. This surely could not be happening to me. I did try and put a brave face on it before I was winched up, but once I was inside the helicopter I just broke my heart. At the time I really didn't think I'd see all my friends again until Southampton. They looked so small, in such a big sea."

Unlike Kinast, Jenkins recovered sufficiently to rejoin the fleet in Wellington. But, as she considered an uncertain future, she began to realize what the race represented. She had struggled to scrape the money together to compete. She sold everything of any value she owned, organized garden fetes and dinner parties. She participated in sponsored cycle rides, and a ten-kilometre fun run. She was consciously investing in a chance to reshape her life, and the pollution she had witnessed

on the first leg down to Rio, convinced her to abandon catering for a career in environmental science.

Ironically enough, the crew she left behind became embroiled in what amounted to an eighty-mile match race to be first around the Horn with *Save the Children*, the other short-handed yacht. *Global Teamwork* had held a thirty-mile lead as she surged down the coast, past the snow-capped mountains of Tierra del Fuego. Skipper Merfyn Owen took the bold option of the short cut through the notorious Le Maire Strait, where the confluence of a wicked westerly wind and a frighteningly strong tide can produce sufficiently violent seas to swallow a container ship, whole. Owen, on the helm, then steered her inshore, anticipating a windshift that never materialized. Hindley seized his chance and, at 07.01 GMT on 3 December, crossed 067.15 W, the official line of Cape Horn. His cheers, carried over the airwaves during the subsequent position report, had a cruel ring on *Teamwork*, beaten by a mere sixteen minutes.

Yet the westerly gales denied everyone something. Unlike in the previous race, where we were able to sail within 400 metres of the shore on the loneliest Cape, the BT Global Challenge boats were pushed up to 100 miles south. Their land-

mark was a GPS navigational reading of a line of longitude. Mine was a line of forbidding cliffs, pockmarked by deep caves that act as nesting sites for a bewildering variety of birdlife. The Horn has the air of a sacred burial site. It commands visitors to commune with its ghosts, and even the BT fleet felt its force. Simon Montague, on *Nuclear Electric*, wrote: "We are now all Cape Horners. Our rounding has in some ways been a bit of an anti-climax, because there was no prospect of seeing that infamous headland, but the seas have taken on a new scale. They are mountains now, rolling hilltops of white foam spewing spray which lashes against our drysuits."

Tudor had taken *Nuclear Electric* on a conservative route, to the east of Staten Island. This involved extra miles, but avoided the lottery of Le Maire. According to Montague, his approach was summed up by a crew briefing as the weather worsened. "You guys must helm so we minimize the shockloads when we're in big seas. Something could break at any time." Wise words, on entry into an alien world. The culture shock of sustained storm force winds should not be underestimated. As music teacher Alan Sears, on *Toshiba*, put it: "It's very wearing, a grind. Imagine living in your bathroom, at an angle of 45°. You get up four times a day, and have freezing water thrown over

LEFT: *SAVE THE CHILDREN*'S BOW TORPEDOEING AS SHE BREAKS THROUGH THE BACK OF A WAVE.

RIGHT: SLEEPING ARRANGEMENTS ON *NUCLEAR ELECTRIC* IN THE SOUTHERN OCEAN. INFORMAL, TO SAY THE LEAST.

RIGHT: Fashion parade on *Nuclear Electric*. Crewman Simon Montague described "rolling hilltops of white foam spewing spray which lashes against our drysuits".

you for hours at a time. Oh, and the ground is constantly moving beneath you. . ." His arched eyebrows rendered any further discussion meaningless.

Toshiba, sixth around the Horn, were chasing *Group 4*, *Motorola* and *Concert*. Simon Walker reported: "The sea is icy and the spray can bring tears to your eyes. Survival and comfort below decks is a matter of wedging yourself in wherever possible, and continuously bracing yourself as the boat falls off wave after wave, crashing down with a thud." On *3Com*, Jane Corfield observed: "There must be worse places on earth, but I can't imagine any right now". On *Group 4*, where conditions were likened to "living in a Moulinex blender", Grahame Gibson was in philosophical form. "It's either heaven or hell" he said. "It's all about total extremes. One minute you're sailing in relatively flat water, with an unbelieveable iceberg out on the horizon. The next you're in a black forty-five-knot squall sent by the devil. Hailstones are in your eyes. You're thinking to yourself 'what am I doing here?' On balance, it's more hell than heaven."

With typical perversity, the pain was increased by a twenty-four-hour respite. Hindley had just lost the lead to Golding, when *Save the Children* was becalmed, when he poured out his frustrations over the yacht's Inmarsat system. "I hate it when there's no wind" he wrote. "Where are we? Calmsville, South Atlantic. Why do we punish ourselves this way? Why do we work for three or four years, getting ready for this chance, and then subject ourselves to the torments and fickleness of nature?" No wonder Merfyn Owen, on *Global Teamwork*, pondered the "mind games" of endurance. Mark Lodge, on *Motorola*, was in prescient mood. He observed: "There's an unerring sense that we should make the most of

ABOVE: WET AND UNCOMFORTABLE WORK ON THE FOREDECK OF *SAVE THE CHILDREN* AS CREW CHANGE THE HEADSAIL WHILE A WAVE BREAKS OVER THEM.

LEFT: A CREWMAN ON *SAVE THE CHILDREN* TAKING A TUMBLE INTO THE REEFED MAINSAIL.

RIGHT: *MOTOROLA* FORGING ON AS PART OF THE LEADING GROUP; HER SKIPPER FELT THE WORST WEATHER AND SEA CONDITIONS WERE YET TO COME.

LEFT AND BELOW LEFT: THE *CONCERT* CREW ASSESSING THE DAMAGE AND MAKING ORDER OUT OF THE CHAOS FOLLOWING THE YACHT'S DISMASTING.

RIGHT: LIKE A LIMB IN PLASTER, A BREAK INVITES GRAFFITI AND THESE OFFERINGS ON THE BROKEN MAST REVEAL THE CREW'S GOOD HUMOUR UNDIMMED BY THE SETBACK.

these past few hours, before the wrath of the Southern Ocean really hits us."

Hindley regained the lead four days later, and, after three and a half weeks at sea, he was first through the Concert Gate, an electronic waypoint designed to prevent the fleet pushing too far south. It was to prove a Pyrrhic victory. The fleet's nightmare scenario began to unfold when he noticed a broken strand at the lower end of *Save the Children*'s backstay. Owen detected similar damage on *Global Teamwork*, and when *3Com*'s forestay failed the race committee shortened the leg by 700 miles by removing another waypoint, which had prevented them setting a direct course for Wellington. Five yachts were to suffer partial or total forestay failure. Four endured failure of the lower stays on the starboard side, a more ominous problem.

The British Steel race had been bedevilled by the weakness of rigging screws. Now the 14mm wire stays were taking such sustained punishment they were aging ten times faster than expected. There was an awful logic about the crisis which faced Chris Tibbs at 17.25 GMT on 18 December, when *Concert*'s mast snapped just above the first spreaders. The only warning was a sickening bang. The boat lurched unnaturally upright, and the upper section of the mast, entangled in a potentially lethal web of shattered steel wire, hung limply over the side. After twenty fruitless minutes, during which the crew attempted to salvage as much as possible for a jury rig, it was still threatening to damage the hull and the rudder. Consequently, it was cut away, and consigned to the icy water.

BROKEN MAST!!
Couldn't stand
the RIGger of
Southern Ocean!
Naomi

Southampton·Rio·Chatham Is.·Wellington
Tilbo's
Unique World
Tour left......
Adnan

FOR SALE
ONE CAREFUL OWNER
11,000 MILES
SLIGHTLY DAMAGED
ANY OFFERS
Richard.

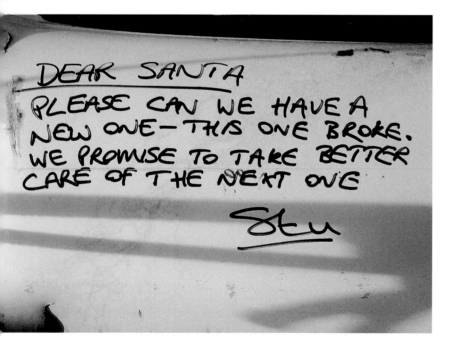

DEAR SANTA
PLEASE CAN WE HAVE A
NEW ONE – THIS ONE BROKE.
WE PROMISE TO TAKE BETTER
CARE OF THE NEXT ONE
Stu

For Tibbs, who had just gone below to snatch some much needed sleep when the incident occurred, it was the end of a uniquely traumatic twenty-four hours. He had been sailing cautiously, in winds receding slowly from a peak of forty-five knots, with three reefs in the mainsail. His priority had been to stabilize the boat after two worrying accidents. John Keating had been the first victim. He was swept across the boat by a wave which obliterated the foredeck, and managed to crawl back into the cockpit before he passed out. Initial fears that he had broken his leg were unjustified, but he still suffered severe muscle damage. He was tied into his bunk when Naomi Kennard was also consumed by a rogue wave, which sprang out of a confused sea. She was picked up, and landed face first on the spinnaker pole.

"I just lay there stunned" she recalled. "I was so glad to feel someone's hand on the back of my neck, dragging me out of trouble." She had two black eyes, and was resting when the mast broke. As a rigger, she understood instantly what had happened. Brian Beaumont was also off watch, but responded immediately to the call for all hands. "As soon as you lose the mast the boat becomes completely unstable" he said. " You get thrown this way and that. We had to learn the rudiments of stability all over again. The galley was a nightmare. Cups were

going. Plates were going. It was awful. You needed four hands." Sea-sickness, made worse by the all-pervading smell of the diesel fuel that represented a lifeline, was soon to return. "The emotions didn't really kick in until much later" reflected Stuart Pask. "First we had practical problems to deal with. But then, a couple of hours later, we hit a real downer. We realized we were out of the race."

The impact on the rest of the fleet was profound. On *Nuclear Electric*, all eyes were on Tudor, who was told of the dismasting by Peter Calvin. "The look on Richard's face was just one of total horror" observed Walters. Tudor was transported back four years, in a fraction of a second. "Uncanny" he said. "It came two days after our anniversary. My heart went out to them, because I knew what they were going through. There's the shock of realizing you are thousands of miles from land. The realization that, after cutting the mast away, your chance of winning the race has gone. You're thankful that no one's been killed or seriously injured, but there's a terrible emptiness." A well rehearsed rescue plan swung into action, led by Lodge, who diverted *Motorola*, but, inevitably, Blyth became embroiled in a safety debate.

"I have suffered all my life from people who tell me what I'm doing is foolhardy" he said. "Generally speaking, they are namby pambies who are not sport orientated. The fact of the

ABOVE: Running repairs to the rigging after problems developed on *Save the Children*'s backstay.

LEFT: Skipper Merfyn Owen making repairs to *Global Teamwork*'s backstay.

RIGHT, TOP AND BOTTOM: *Motorola* assisting *Concert* with a handover of fuel.

FAR RIGHT: *Concert* enters the relative safety of the Chatham Islands for her refuel en route to Wellington.

matter is that a man or woman wants a challenge, wants adventure. They understand what is involved and are prepared to run with it. They've been pushing the yachts very very hard. It is a reasonable assumption, in a one-design race, that once something goes wrong on one boat it will go wrong on the rest. The last time we had the problem with rigging screws. Now the problem has moved to the next weakest link in the chain. I do feel for the crews. I selected them myself and identify with their ambitions. They'll just pick themselves up, dust themselves down, and get on with it."

Lodge consulted Golding, who had gone to Tudor's aid four years previously, on the delicate art of making a fuel transfer. It was a misty morning when *Motorola* spotted *Concert*, which looked as helpless as a bird with a broken wing. "The initial reaction in those circumstances is shock, really" he noted. "It's emotional, seeing a crippled yacht, miles from anywhere. But you can't afford to dwell on it. You've a job to do." Over the course of eight hours, he transferred 120 gallons, in yellow containers. His crew donated a bottle of Famous Grouse scotch before they responded to his call for three cheers. *Courtaulds* and *Time & Tide* were to make similar contact, but nothing was as moving as that first farewell. "There was not a dry eye on the boat" stressed Tibbs. "We were envious. They had something we didn't. A mast."

The Southern Ocean veterans in the fleet had similar reactions. Hindley was on deck when the news broke, and rushed below to speak to Owen, on duty yacht *Global Teamwork*. "Merv" he implored "Please tell me it's not happened." He admitted to being "shellshocked". Walker, on *Toshiba*, was struck by a sudden sense of responsibility. "You're immediately aware of your own vulnerability" he said. "It dawns on you that people could be seriously hurt in the middle of nowhere. You think

'that could be us', but then you just get on with your job. You do your best, and hope it's good enough." On *Heath Insured II*, however, Adrian Donovan's sympathy soured.

He was angered when *Heath* came within a split second of losing her rig in identical circumstances to *Concert*. The mast moved eighteen inches out of line when her inner stay was left hanging by four of its nineteen strands. "I thought 'here we go again'" he said. "There was this horrible sense of déjà vu. I

couldn't believe that after all the structural work done after the British Steel race, we faced the prospect of being stuck down there again." He sat at the chart table and composed a confidential message, which was duly leaked to the Press. His view, that the race should have been stopped and judged on positions taken at the Concert Gate, was provocative enough. But to be quoted as calling the race "a farce" invited a reaction from Blyth.

He denied speculation that he was about to sack Donovan, but confirmed he would "be having a word with him" when he arrived in Wellington. "You can't make those type of accusations and not get any fall out" he said. "I can't remember the last time a yacht race was stopped. Even the Fastnet, in the year of the deaths, continued. I can't accept criticism like that, and not be expected to respond." Donovan, meanwhile, was nonplussed by what he considered a manufactured controversy. "I made no official observations to anyone" he insisted. "I just had ideas in my head. We were in a dangerous situation, sailing boats which had developed serious problems. The sea never changes. You can get too blasé about it, and we have a duty to our crews to be responsible."

Hatfield, meanwhile, was being given another indication of the depth of his commitment to a disabled crew. He had been forced to rendezvous with Donovan to pick up more painkillers for Brendan West, an amputee who joined the crew in Rio along with cancer sufferer Mike Austin, a British Airways pilot. West's left leg had been removed after a hit and run accident in 1979. The knee of his reconstructed right leg was badly broken midway across the Southern Ocean, when mate Chris Ogg, propelled by a huge wave in a fifty-knot storm, fell on it. He was whimpering in agony as he was helped below, down a

RIGHT: *GROUP 4* APPROACHING A MIST-LADEN NEW ZEALAND ON THE HORIZON.

ABOVE: *3Com* APPROACHES
WELLINGTON.

RIGHT: LOW MIST THREATENS TO
ENVELOP *MOTOROLA* AS SHE ENDS
THE LEG.

FAR RIGHT: TRIUMPHANT SKIPPER
JAMES HATFIELD (REAR)
CELEBRATING *TIME & TIDE*'S
PERFORMANCE ON THE LEG.

chute constructed out of soaking sailcloth. He then endured the indignity of having his trousers cut off, before he was tied into his bunk for three excruciatingly painful weeks.

"I thought the pain would ease in a few minutes" he said. "They tied my legs together, gave me a happy pill to shut me up, and for ten days I thought I'd only sustained severe bruising. Eventually, all I could do was writhe around." Even amongst a group of people with habitually high pain thresholds, he was admired. As Paul Burns observed: "We all felt for him. He tried to conceal just how much it was hurting. But you only had to look at his face, when the boat slammed off a wave, to know the full story." *Time & Tide* were racing with two men short, because John Rich, a victim of stomach cancer, was suffering from a sustained fever.

Golding's problems were minimal by comparison, but *Group 4*'s serene progress towards their second successive win was becoming a little too serene. As the pursuing pack dealt

with the remnants of Hurricane Fergus, they were becalmed at the mouth of Wellington harbour. In one infuriating seven-hour overnight spell, they floated a mile forward, a mile and a half sideways, and a mile backwards. The beauty of the sunrise, which merged slashes of orange with delicate shades of pink and lemon, was lost on Timon Robson as he catnapped on the windward rail. "Everyone's been awake for getting on for twenty-four hours" he complained. "We're dead on our feet. People are grumpy. We all know *Save the Children* are piling up behind us. It's like some form of torture."

He need not have worried. The wind filled in and, as Hindley's yacht appeared on the horizon, *Group 4* heard the welcome retort of the finishing cannon. It was then, and only then, that Golding could acknowledge the strains of leadership. "I felt as if I was sitting on a timebomb" he said. "I spent a lot of time out there worrying. It's a real battle, because you have to find a subtle compromise between pushing hard and

breaking things. You never really find the right balance. If you lose miles to other boats you feel you're not pushing hard enough. But if you gain miles you're probably pushing too hard. You've got to be totally committed to this race on a personal basis. All the crew have gone through a lot of discomfort on this leg. You have to accept the risk of injury is very high. The potential for disaster is always there. As a skipper, when you make decisions you have to be convinced your crew will be safe."

Golding commanded a respect bordering on awe from those around him. They accepted limitations on their lives, such as his insistence that Christmas would not be celebrated formally until they reached New Zealand. This made *Group 4* unique in the fleet, who compensated for their isolation from friends and family by attempting to recreate the spirit of home and hearth in cold, unseasonal galleys. They had enduring memories of carols, played through deck speakers, on a moonlit Christmas night. *Group 4* had another Courtaulds Trophy, as leg winners. "For us, Christmas didn't exist" confirmed Andrea Bacon. "It was just another day on the racing calendar. It was a non event, but Mike told us it would eventually take place in Wellington. There are no days off with him. He's very disciplined. We heard everyone else talking about what they were eating, and what presents they had received. To

LEFT: A CHAMPAGNE SHOWER AT THE HANDS OF RICHARD TUDOR AND HIS *NUCLEAR ELECTRIC* TEAM.

BELOW LEFT: *GROUP 4* SKIPPER MIKE GOLDING CHATS TO THE CAPED CRUSADERS FROM *MOTOROLA* DOING THEIR OWN BIT OF REFUELLING.

ABOVE RIGHT: BRENDAN WEST BEING STRETCHERED OFF TO THE CHEERS OF FELLOW *TIME & TIDE* CREW MEMBERS.

ABOVE, FAR RIGHT: A GAUNT LOOKING JOHN RICH, ALSO OF *TIME & TIDE*, MANAGING TO WALK TO HIS AMBULANCE AT THE END OF THE LEG.

RIGHT: A TRADITIONAL MAORI WELCOME FOR THE PARTICIPANTS.

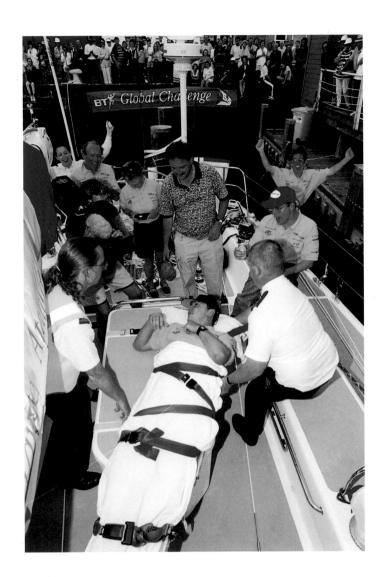

be honest, by the end of the day I was relieved to get into Boxing Day."

Hindley, who had made up thirty-five miles overnight, was also relieved, but radiating frustration. He felt the rigging problems had denied him victory, and sought compensation in the unifying nature of collective sacrifice. "This has brought the crew together" he suggested. "It has given them an insight into themselves. They're stronger than when they left Southampton. They've developed an ability to cope." It was a lesson of uniform importance. *Motorola* finished third on corrected time, after they had been given an allowance of just under nine hours for their assistance of *Concert*. The Southern Ocean might have

welded Lodge's crew together spiritually, but Valerie Bell, the American nurse who acted as yacht medic, had a word for it. "It was just awful, very awful" she said, an arresting sight in the team's arrival outfit of black cape and bat-mask. "I expected it to be awful and it was awful. There were some good points, like sailing along with the sun glistening on the water, and it was something I probably had to go through, to prove something to myself. But, as Mark says, anyone who says they enjoy the Southern Ocean is either lying, nuts, or they've never really been there. It was awful."

As she went off, to get drunk for only the second time in her life, the fleet began to reassemble. Three boats arrived on New Year's Eve, as 10,000 people attended a rock concert in the harbour complex, but the biggest welcome, as ever, was reserved for *Time & Tide*. They fulfilled their ambition by finishing eleventh, ahead of the able-bodied crews on *Courtaulds International*, *Heath Insured II* and *Concert*. Hatfield, for one, was reduced to tears. "I never thought we had so many friends,

so many people who believed in us" he said, as the crew's theme tune, "Simply the Best" by Tina Turner, blared out over the public address system. "My guys were brilliant. But there are two more down below, who are suffering and can't see this. They deserve to be up here alongside us, because everyone is in this together."

As if on cue, Rich, hauntingly thin and hesitant, was helped to the waiting ambulance by Paul Hebblethwaite, his deaf colleague. As West emerged on a stretcher, clutching a bottle of champagne under one arm and a four-can pack of lager under the other, the crowd lining the harbour walls broke into a spontaneous chorus of "For He's a Jolly Good Fellow". A trite anthem, maybe, but on this sunny Southern Hemisphere evening it had relevance beyond ritual. The sight of his artificial leg, sticking out of his overnight bag, was an arresting symbol of a group of people, making others concentrate on their abilities, rather than their disabilities. " What we'll never have is the natural strength of the other crews" Austin reflected. "Sail changes in heavy weather are absolutely horrendous. But I look around and I see a pretty special bunch of people. It's been a privilege to see us come together in the hard times."

The same could be said of the *Concert* crew, who spent a suitably bizarre New Year's Eve on the Chatham Islands, a crayfish-producing outpost 400 miles east of New Zealand. Tudor was one of the first to greet them when they motored into Wellington on 3 January, flying a cannibalized spinnaker from their jury rig. The crew gathered in the forepeak area, sipped beer, and laughed. Private sadness could wait. A new mast would be fitted in Wellington, and they still had each other. "We might not be able to win overall" skipper Tibbs reflected. "But we're not finished yet." He was inordinately proud. His crew knew the answers to those predictable questions now. Yes they had been scared, cold, tired and hungry. War stories, fresh off the press, were ready to be embroidered.

LEFT: THE *CONCERT* CREW CELEBRATING NEW YEAR'S EVE IN THE ONLY HOTEL BAR IN THE CHATHAM ISLANDS WITH FRIENDS AND FAMILY FLOWN IN FROM NEW ZEALAND.

ABOVE: RICHARD TUDOR OF *NUCLEAR ELECTRIC* ESCORTS *CONCERT* INTO WELLINGTON. HE HAD LOST HIS MAST ABOARD *BRITISH STEEL II* IN THE PREVIOUS CHALLENGE.

RIGHT: HOME IS THE HERO. HOME FROM THE SEA.

Boats That Go Bump in the Night

1,230 miles

The Maori tribal elder looked as if he had swallowed a wasp. His eyes bulged and, as he bowed his head, he emitted a low groan which suggested he was gargling with volcanic lava. He might have given the impression of preparing to enter a bar room brawl, but he was on the foredeck of the yacht *Motorola*, blessing the boat. It was a simple ceremony, completed when he mingled among the crew, who stood in a semi-circle around him. He gave each of us a fish hook made out of fish bone, a traditional good luck talisman, together with a fern, a powerful symbol of everlasting life. There was an immediate, unspoken agreement not to tempt fate and incur *tapu*, misfortune.

LEFT: PICTURE POSTCARD SETTING OF THE SYDNEY OPERA HOUSE, THE FINISH LINE FOR LEG THREE FROM WELLINGTON, THE SHORTEST OF THE RACE. SYDNEY HARBOUR WAS CALLED THE "FINEST HARBOUR IN THE WORLD" BY ITS DISCOVERER, CAPT. ARTHUR PHILLIP. THE MODERN WATERFRONT OFFERS A PERFECT BACKDROP FOR *HEATH INSURED II*.

To this day I wear the tokens around my neck, together with the small St Christopher medallion that my mother insisted I take around the world four years previously.

Chay Blyth might have characterized the 1,250-mile third leg of the BT Global Challenge, from Wellington to Sydney, as "no more than a hop, skip and a jump", but there was no point in unnecessary risk. Over the previous 12,000 miles the crews had developed a healthy respect for the sea. This had been emphasized during the protracted stopover in New Zealand, by television coverage of the Southern Ocean rescue operations involving Tony Bullimore, who survived for four days in his upturned yacht, and Pete Goss, who saved Frenchman Raphael Dinelli from certain death. Goss, particularly, was close to the BT fleet, and the impact of his heroism, recognized by France's highest honour, the Legion d'honneur, was appreciated by *Motorola*'s Mark Lodge, who had the misfortune to be my skipper for the duration.

"Perhaps we all needed a wake-up call" he mused as we eased out into Lambton Bay, to work through pre-start manoeuvres. "We've been off the boats for five weeks, but all

Pete's problems, and the footage we've seen of Bullimore's rescue, brings it home. You can never over-emphasize the pressure that the sea exerts on people. That tends to come out in frustration and fear. In normal life, you are rarely in a situation where you are truly scared, but in this race people have willingly put themselves in that position. It can have a dramatic effect. People become fearful to the point of sobbing. It takes courage to admit you are scared because everyone has a certain image of assurance they like to project. But if that admission makes everyone more conscious of the dangers, it's no bad thing. There are personality clashes on all boats. It's inevitable to a certain extent because you have fourteen different characters thrown together in stressful circumstances they can't escape from. It's instructive to learn about people's abilities and shortcomings, but it's difficult to gauge exactly how much they've changed since they left Southampton because everyone is cocooned in this tight little world."

The philosophical approach was appropriate. The fleet took stock of itself on the other side of the world. Each boat had been meticulously rerigged after the traumas of the second leg, and it slowly dawned on the amateur sailors that they were involved in a global phenomenon. More than 1,000 British schools were using the race, within the context of the national curriculum, to learn about the world. They sent drawings to each yacht, and asked wonderfully innocent questions – "what are whales like?" – by e-mail. By the time the yachts reached Sydney there had been more than twenty million hits on the BT Global Challenge internet site, which was being updated four times a day. The Challenge was being given shape and substance by interviews, photographs and video clips, all transmitted on the worldwide web. Callers logged in from the Caribbean to the Czech Republic, from Ecuador to Estonia. Another 3,000 people were staging their own virtual yacht race, which was emulating the fleet's "wrong way" circumnavigation.

The relative sprint across the Tasman Sea had been identified as "the chairman's leg", a chance for executives to discover, at first hand, the people power of an event that fitted into their marketing plans. Nuclear Electric chairman Mark Baker looked forward to swapping "the comfort of the boardroom for the hurly-burly of a narrow bunk". Dr Alan Rudge, BT's deputy chief executive, sailed on *Global Teamwork*. *Ocean Rover* recruited Prince Michael of Kent, who attended the start in Southampton and was persuaded to compete after watching the finish in Rio, where he was involved in a trade mission to Brazil. Michael Buerk, the BBC newsreader, joined Simon Walker on *Toshiba*. He admitted to being "knackered" after a single training session. Lodge obviously got the short end of the straw. A hack tottering off the plane from London, where he had been sampling the social excesses of Five Nations rugby. At least, I assured myself, sea-sickness would be no problem. I never suffered on the previous race. There would only be a week, at most, between parties. My diary of the leg, which

FAR LEFT: HRH PRINCE MICHAEL OF KENT WAVING GOOD-BYE TO WELLINGTON FROM *OCEAN ROVER*. HE HAD JUST JOINED THE CREW FOR THE LEG TO SYDNEY.

LEFT: THE YACHTS SAIL OUT OF WELLINGTON CONVENIENTLY ALIGNED AT THE START OF LEG THREE.

LEFT: *COURTAULDS INTERNATIONAL* WITH *GROUP 4* CLOSE BY AT THE START IN WELLINGTON.

follows, is the story of an accident waiting to happen, interspersed by daily reality checks.

Sunday 9 Feb: Woken at 4am by soft drink cans clattering down deserted street. Incessant rain is being driven against the windowpane by a strong wind. So much for TV predictions of a bright and brisk day. Forget to take my Stugeron tablets, as insurance against sea-sickness, but, hey, what's the problem? A chaotic start, as anticipated. We lose out in the scrum at the second turning mark, but accelerate through the fleet after leaving Wellington harbour. As light begins to fade, a fateful decision. Instead of pushing inshore, towards New Zealand's North Island, we opt to head for the opposite coast. Only time will tell whether we have unwittingly surrendered the initiative. **Reality Check:** We have. The agenda is being set by Adrian Donovan, on *Heath Insured II*, Andy Hindley, on *Save the Children*, and Richard Tudor, who spectacularly blew *Nuclear Electric*'s spinnaker. *Motorola* drop from fourth to eleventh, but only ten miles separate leaders *Heath* and *Time & Tide*, who are last.

Monday 10 Feb: I can't believe this. An unwanted reminder of the subtle stresses of sea-sickness, which extend beyond the indignities of ritual regurgitation. Nausea strips you of self-esteem, entices you into withdrawing into yourself. Swathed in a storm suit, hanging over the guard rail, you become silently obsessed by your plight. You are dehydrated and acutely conscious of a noxious taste at the back of your

throat. It is a temporary affliction but for forty-eight hours it feels like an alien has invaded your digestive tract, which it is prodding with knitting needles. No wonder Valerie Bell has abandoned the race. Sea-sickness confined her to her bunk for three weeks on the last leg. Still wept buckets when we left, though. "That's my family" she wailed as we slipped the mooring lines. **Reality check:** *Heath* still leads. Boris Webber takes the gamble of heading north on *Courtaulds International*, and trails the fleet by thirty-two miles.

Tuesday 11 Feb: A menacing moonless night. Storm force winds toy with the boat, making life barely bearable both on and below deck. You are reduced to a crab-like scuttle in the cockpit or in your cabin. Sleep is elusive, although you are exhausted. You become accustomed to being jolted awake by momentary weightlessness when the yacht falls off a wave with a resonant thud. Crew member John Aitchison is thrown out of his bunk by one particularly violent jolt. Little does he know it, but the incident is a foretaste of things to come. Feel so wretched I decide to break out my Pampers, the one luxury item

allowed on board. They're the baby wipes which refresh the parts others dare not reach. **Reality check:** *Motorola* are ninth. On the western edge of the fleet Mike Golding, on *Group 4*, is rewarded for waiting for the wind to back. He flies a spinnaker, into first place.

Wednesday 12 Feb: The charts tell us we are well into the Tasman Sea but it feels like the North Sea. The clouds are uniformly grey, and the sea has a flat metallic colour. The saving grace is that the water is not as cold as in a northern hemisphere winter, and the wind is appreciably warmer. Competitively we are in no-man's land, oscillating between eighth and tenth place. But the racing is so close – we can see up to nine other yachts as the sea mellows – it leads to the triumph of optimism over experience. Alternative entertainment is provided by TV lawyer Ben Challis, a novice sailor who has more in common with Charlie Chaplin than Chay Blyth. His graphic description of attempting to go to the toilet in a storm – "little boys need a hand free to pee" – is a classic. **Reality check:** *Group 4* lead, forty-six miles ahead of *Courtaulds*, who remain last.

RIGHT: A SPECTACULAR BIRDS-EYE VIEW OF *COURTAULDS INTERNATIONAL*.

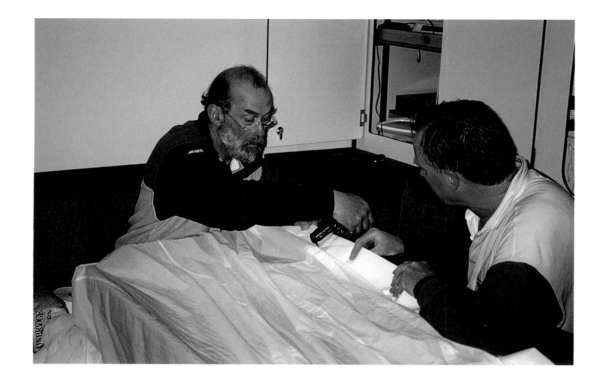

Save the Children drop to tenth, as Hindley heads north with the intention of skirting a high-pressure system.

Thursday 13 Feb: Death watch, the four-hour stint served on alternative nights between 2 and 6 am, claims its customary victims. A wave sweeps the foredeck during a sail change to a number two yankee, and two crew members sustain typical injuries. Rob Chatwin twists his knee as he rushes to the aid of Aitchison, who is pinned against the forestay by the force of the water. Thank God he had clipped on. John must be missing his Newcastle hotel. He's already suffering from a stomach injury sustained on the last leg, and feels faint. He has suspected broken ribs, so I help him to shuffle to the heads, where medic Kevin Smythe, who joined the crew in Wellington, takes a urine sample. He is sufficiently concerned to test for internal bleeding. **Reality check:** With 500 miles to go, *Group 4* and *Heath* are holding station at the head of the fleet. The race is a lottery, with the search for wind being conducted across a ninety-two-mile band from *Save the Children*, in the north, to *Commercial Union*, who are furthest south.

Friday 14 Feb: Valentine's Day. Thank the Lord for Interflora. Aitchison is making a steady recovery, and may be suffering only from severe bruising. His progress mirrors the upbeat mood of the yacht, which is accelerating nicely under spinnaker. Still no sun. So instead of working on the body beautiful, we concentrate on the power of our imaginations. Truncated sleep patterns have been producing some vivid and bizarre dreams. Shark sightings lead me into a *Yellow Submarine* fantasy. I am sailing with the Beatles and swimming with psychedelic sharks in a multi-coloured sea. Ben Challis dreams his dog is being butchered. Steve Wyre, another *Motorola* legger, imagines he is a ghostly presence in a Victorian child's

playroom. Time for the reality of land methinks. **Reality check:** *Concert* have moved up to second. *Ocean Rover* inform race HQ that their crew is either "too old or too unattractive" to receive messages of undying love. They also hope that we didn't see them blow their 1.5oz spinnaker in our tacking duel. Fat chance. . .

     Saturday 15 Feb: If only life were simple. Another day which summarizes the schizophrenia of ocean racing. A wild ride under spinnaker through persistent squalls until mid-afternoon is intoxicating. Being on the edge of control stirs basic instincts, and leaves the crew wide eyed. But, just as suddenly as the thirty-five knot winds had appeared, they vanish. As darkness falls the southern half of the fleet compresses into a bunch. We bob abjectly around like rubber ducks in a baby's bathwater. Seek a sense of perspective by remembering the plight of Sean Blowers, forced off *Commercial Union* with back problems. I've sent him to a contact at the Australian Academy of Sport for make or break treatment, but it is not looking good. A sobering thought as we pass the night, sitting and squirming on the windward rail. I know it's not an original line, but I've "Gotta Get Out Of This Place". **Reality check:** Tom O'Connor, on *Pause to Remember*, reports that "it feels as if the boats are getting ready for the start". Seven miles span the first eleven boats, but Hindley is holding his breath. We are not to know it, but he's picked up the wind first.

Sunday 16 Feb: Dawn reveals the extent of the havoc inflicted by the flat calm. Some boats are drifting sideways. Others are going backwards. One, *Toshiba*, is alongside us, pirouetting like a drunken ballet dancer. The wind fills in slowly, reluctantly. It unleashes a fifteen-hour drag race between eight yachts that climaxes in a bizarre incident which will live with us forever. We are surging towards the entrance to Sydney Harbour, in driving rain, when our flanker explodes. Cue carnage. Lodge, on the helm attempting to hold off *Toshiba*, implores us to retrieve the remnants of the sail. "Go on lads" he shouts. "Get it back. You're saving us four hours." It is pitch black. Electrical problems mean we have no instruments. "Have we got water?" Lodge yells. Navigator John Crozier is climbing the steps, with a warning, when we hit the South Reef, which guards the harbour entrance. Challis is a blue blur, flying horizontally across the deck. Aitchison reinjures his ribs. Chatwin is hit full in the face by a flailing rope. A stunned silence is broken by Lodge's laughter. "This is ridiculous" he exclaims. "I'm going to get slaughtered for this. Hey, Calvin, did I get you a story, or what?" **Reality check:** *Motorola*, which slipped off the reef when the crew shifted its collective weight to the foredeck, finish eleventh, and remain fourth overall. Eleven yachts cross the line over a two and a half hour period, and less than six hours separate winners *Save the Children* from last placed *Time & Tide. Group 4* finish second, just ahead of *Courtaulds International*, who gain late reward for Webber's tactical gamble.

Monday 17 Feb: No one shows the remotest interest in going to bed. Michael Buerk hangs over the pulpit of *Toshiba*, munching a meat pie and swigging VB beer from a litre bottle. His face is drawn. His clothes are dishevelled. He reflects: "It was bloody uncomfortable. The food was absolutely appalling, reconstituted nothing. But it was kind of exhilarating. The ladies in the crew said it was like childbirth. You only remember the best bits afterwards. I was willing. That's as far as I go as a sailor, but I'm glad I've done it." Just along Darling Harbour,

LEFT, TOP: JUBILATION ABOARD *COURTAULDS INTERNATIONAL* AFTER THEIR THIRD PLACE FINISH.

LEFT: *3COM* FILMING THEIR OWN ARRIVAL CELEBRATIONS AT DARLING HARBOUR.

RIGHT: THE PRIZE GIVING IN SYDNEY ATTRACTED THOUSANDS FOR THE BIG PARTY.

Prince Michael of Kent is resisting the protocol officials who want to immunize him from the madness. "It was really quite special" he says. "The lovely thing is that this gives a generation of Britons the chance to experience adventure." Hindley, wearing a red spotted pirate's bandana, is having difficulty remaining upright. "Unbelievable" he slurs. Even Blyth looks as if he's had a tincture or two. John Swingewood, a BT executive on *Pause to Remember*, suggests, over a chilled Chardonnay, that "this is one of the best things I've ever done". Adrian Donovan,

devastated that his pacemaking had not paid off, promises "I'm going to take up golf". Malcolm McKeag, who had sailed with *Time & Tide*, is exultant. "I'm seriously impressed. What a bunch of people. This has let me into their secret. No one on this boat has a problem with their problem." Everyone adjourns to the all-night pub across the road where a new drink, Motorola on the Rocks, is unveiled at around 4.30am. It's simple, blue curaçao on ice, and far too tasty. **Reality check:** Where am I?

Fear and Loathing in the Fifties

6,200 miles

Imagine, for a moment, that you are a skipper in the BT Global Challenge. You have abandoned the sanctuary of Sydney for the fourth leg of the race, to Cape Town. You have just survived a Southern Ocean storm, and sit down at the computer to update your log of the journey. What you are typing, as you wedge yourself in a corner of the galley with your feet pivoting against the wall, is blurred, indistinct. It is difficult to focus when sleep is routinely rationed to four hours in every twenty-four, largely taken in catnaps. It is impossible to escape the cold, the all-pervading dampness. Your cabin, at the aft of the yacht behind the galley, is awash with condensation.

LEFT: THE SOUTHERN OCEAN WEATHER OFFERED THE MOST TESTING CONDITIONS OF THE ENTIRE RACE. RAGING SEAS COMBINED WITH THE COLD AND WIND TO CREATE ALMOST INTOLERABLE EXPERIENCES; DURING LEG FOUR IT WAS GALE FORCE (ABOUT FORTY KNOTS) FOR OVER HALF THE DURATION, REACHING A HIGH OF SEVENTY-SIX KNOTS.

All you can hear is the on-watch, shouting at each other in a vain attempt to be heard above the cacophony of wind and waves. All you can see is the fear in the eyes of the stand-by watch, who are waiting, fully kitted-up, to attend any emergency. This is what you find yourself writing.

"I watched my 'amateurs' in action last night. One was sitting in the leeward side of the cockpit until a large wall of water fell on him. He went over backwards into the scuppers, where he began to swim like a salmon against the stream. He was swept towards the rail and the waiting Southern Ocean. He had to come past me and in that micro-second I wondered if I could leave the wheel to grab him. Could I have held him? And what of the fate of the others left on deck, exposed to the next breaking sea while the wheel spun free? Fortunately my wayward salmon was brought up short on his safety harness as a second wave tried to finish the task of the first. The salmon lifted himself off his back, coughing and vomiting copious amounts of sea water. I am no wiser as to what I would have done. The questions rattle round my brain, unanswered. I'm only grateful that he has listened to one thing I've said: 'clip on'.

"It's already a past issue. The need is to concentrate on the now – what's happening on deck. Who's where, and where is the next wave, and what's its angle to us? We rise up a massive sea and plunge down into the trough to see a wall of white water breaking aboard. I yell a warning to the deck. My last frame of focussed vision is of the shroud checker, trying to remove the anti-chafe protection from the rigging screw. My world goes white and the wind is knocked out of my body. Water forces its way down my oilskins, up my nose and down my throat. A terrific force is trying to wrench me from the wheel. I feel a panic build inside. How many of my crew are still on deck? In a matter of seconds I sweep the deck, following the destructive path of that wall of water. The rig man – where is he? The shroud is empty and the last picture in my mind had him squatting there. I turn my head to leeward and astern, searching for him in the water. I'm shouting his name. No one seems to respond. It's happened. I've lost a man overboard. I'm still yelling when someone points down and the familiar face grins up from the other side of the mast. Later, I find myself thinking about our friends and relatives. You entrusted the crew into my care. I'm not sure, but I don't think they will be the same people I return to you."

Imagine, then, what *Time & Tide* skipper James Hatfield felt when he submitted that passage in his daily report to race HQ. It was certainly sufficient to silence sanctimonious critics of his disabled crew when it was reproduced in the magazine *Yachting World*. Recruitment problems, exacerbated by a petty dispute which led to the withdrawal of Liz Tring just before the departure from Sydney, meant that he was forced to sail the most demanding section of the Challenge with only twelve crew members, two short. By the time of that first storm, south of Tasmania, where winds reached seventy knots, he was also without one of his key men, Paul Hebblethwaite. His strength and vivacity more than compensated for his deafness, but he had been horribly injured within twenty-four hours of leaving Sydney. He was thrown against a horned metal cleat, the anchor point for one of the many ropes leading into the cock-

pit It pierced his rectum. Internal stitches were inserted as he lay on the galley table, but he was confined to his bunk for long spells. No one had any inclination to argue when he likened the pain to that of childbirth.

Little wonder, then, that a contemplative atmosphere enveloped the crews before they left Darling Harbour. This was the ordeal everyone dreaded. Several crew members, citing the prospect of severe sea-sickness, succumbed to their fears, and flew to Cape Town to await the fleet. Others had more valid

LEFT: CROWDS THRONG THE WATERFRONT AT SYDNEY PRIOR TO THE START OF LEG FOUR.

RIGHT: SIMON WALKER (CENTRE, WITH SUNGLASSES) GIVES HIS *TOSHIBA WAVE WARRIOR* TEAM A PEP TALK BEFORE THE OFF.

BELOW: THE *NUCLEAR ELECTRIC* CREW GIVE "THREE CHEERS" TO SYDNEY AND AUSTRALIA.

reasons to demur. John Aitchison retired from the *Motorola* crew because of the worryingly persistent nature of his rib injuries. *Ocean Rover*'s Paul Stephens, an accountant, missed the leg because of a bizarre accident at the Sydney Aquarium. He had the incalculable misfortune to be walking past a glass shark tank when it exploded, badly cutting his arm, and the muscles which control movement of the wrist and fingers. Sean Blowers returned to England to await back surgery. In general terms, however, those who did set sail were proving an important point to themselves. No one made it more eloquently or emotionally than Christine Burge, a graphic artist from London.

It would have been easy for Christine to give up in Sydney. She had never hidden her terror of the Southern Ocean, and had sobbed for three days in anticipation of rounding Cape Horn on *Motorola*. What happened subsequently defined the wider importance of the BT Global Challenge, the constructive proof of man-management skills it offered. Skipper Mark Lodge spent long spells with her, when the strain seemed to be too

LEFT, TOP: *GROUP 4* AND *COMMERCIAL UNION* IN A MINOR COLLISION AT THE OUTSET OF WHAT WAS A PARTICULARLY ENERGETIC LEG.

LEFT: PERFECT SAILING CONDITIONS AS THE MANOEUVRING FOR POSITION COMMENCES.

RIGHT: PAST THE OLD FORT DENISON IN SYDNEY HARBOUR THE CROSS-TACKING BEGINS AND THE RACE FOR THE HONOUR OF FIRST PAST THE SYDNEY HEADS.

much. "I knew what she was going through" he said. "I wanted her to know that she wasn't alone, that we were there for her." He consoled her, cajoled her. The crew rallied around, convincing her that she had nothing to fear but fear itself. "I hate it, just hate it" she argued. She still loathed the ordeal of heavy weather sailing when we were together, on the short sprint from Wellington, but she had conquered herself. It was a small, private, victory. Inspirational, in the forgotten sense that the sum of the Challenge is greater than the parts of its whole. As Mark Baptist, a watch leader on *Motorola*, wrote in his diary:

"We may wonder why we ever returned to the Southern Ocean, but it is fantastic, an amazing experience. I think deep down we all know we will come out of this stronger individuals, a closer team. We've experienced something most people will never even get a glimpse of."

Any major sports event is a blend of idealism and commercialism. The sponsors inevitably became emotionally involved with crews, because respect and admiration are the common currency of round the world yacht races. But the complementary justification for their investment came in the form

LEFT: *OCEAN ROVER* WENDS HER
WAY OUT PAST SYDNEY HARBOUR
BRIDGE CLOSELY FOLLOWED BY
PAUSE TO REMEMBER.

of the unique business opportunity the BT Global Challenge represented. It was a networker's dream. Everyone, from the title sponsor through the fourteen individual boat sponsors to the 180 companies enlisted as business club members, had a common interest. Many of the backers, such as Motorola, Toshiba, Digital and the consortium of companies involved with the Global Teamwork project, were keen to use the event to strengthen long-term business partnerships with BT. Sponsors had the opportunity to organize business events in every port of call to showcase their technologies and develop local business relationships. Sydney's regional importance lay in its proximity to the Asia-Pacific marketplace.

But that only represented several parts of a much bigger jigsaw puzzle. Typically, Dr Alan Rudge, the senior executive who emerged as the driving force behind BT's involvement, stepped off *Global Teamwork* in Darling Harbour with an invaluable insight into the wider relevance of the human qualities the race promoted. He suffered from sea-sickness, watched those around him come to terms with their own weaknesses, and then put the experience into the context of a global company, conducting operations in thirty countries. "It wasn't exactly fun" he acknowledged. "It really tested me. It gives you an idea of what your limits are, and whether you can go beyond them. To give an example, when you have to get up in the middle of the night to go on watch, and you're feeling tired and your muscles are aching, to pull on oilies and go up on deck takes some doing. But if you can get through it, you get a marvellous sense of achievement, and your confidence grows. It's teamwork that makes all the difference on a racing yacht and in business. Your effort, combined with that of your fellow crew members, is what makes the difference. You are all pulling together to achieve the same goal."

Given that perspective, the pomposity of the response by the sailing authorities to some of the emotions released by the start gun in Sydney was puzzling. Boris Webber, *Courtaulds* skipper, was threatened with severe disciplinary action when a viewer of the BBC TV documentary series objected to the manner in which he berated an inattentive weekend sailor, who nearly collided with his yacht in the hurly-burly of the start sequence. Webber was eventually given a reprimand, but only after being subjected to the unnecessary inconvenience of being asked to prepare for an official hearing in Germany, a week before the start of the final leg from Boston. The Southern Ocean imposes its own code of conduct, which has little relevance to the cosy clubbability of the committee room. An emotional dam burst when the BT fleet raced past the Sydney Opera House. The skippers were like boxers emerging from their corner, before the sound of the first bell has subsided. Scared, but strangely secure in the knowledge that their punishment would be sustained, severe, and unavoidable. The pent up nervous energy, stimulated by the prospect of returning to a uniquely inhospitable environment, resulted in five protest flags being

flown. Before the adrenalin rush had subsided, *Group 4* had collided with *Commercial Union*, who cut across her bows under pressure. Chay Blyth, who warned crews "you won't have Utopia" in his traditional eve-of-race address, could be forgiven a sardonic smile.

Consider what lay ahead before rushing to premature judgement about temperament or tactics. When the leg was over Andrew Roberts, the project director, made a clinical assessment of what the fleet had endured. The wind was gale force, or beyond, for twenty-eight of the forty-one days they were at sea. It exceeded sixty knots on twelve days, and reached seventy-six knots. Typically, the wind doubled in speed, from twenty-five or thirty knots, in less than three minutes. Crews conducted up to thirteen separate sail changes in twelve-hour spells, when they were beating to windward in temperatures which, when wind chill was taken into account, were as low as minus 30° Centigrade. Six yachts suffered sufficiently severe knockdowns to damage their radar domes, which stand twelve feet above the waterline. There was no significant rigging damage, but stanchions were bent by the force of the water, and three compasses were wrenched off their binnacles. The hull of the yacht *Global Teamwork* was scarred by growlers, submerged lumps of ice, often the size of a semi-detached house, which are the silent assassins of the sea. When the boats

LEFT, TOP: *COURTAULDS INTERNATIONAL*, FIRST PAST THE HEADS.

LEFT, BOTTOM: THE GLOWING SCENE IN BORIS WEBBER'S *COURTAULDS INTERNATIONAL'S* NAVIGATION STATION.

ABOVE RIGHT: READY FOR ACTION ON *TOSHIBA*. AN INSULATED SUIT WAS ESSENTIAL OUT ON DECK.

RIGHT: A WELL WRAPPED MERFYN OWEN AT THE WHEEL ON *GLOBAL TEAMWORK*. HAPPILY HIS NOSE DID NOT DROP OFF IN THE BITTERLY COLD WIND.

reached Cape Town, 101 sails out of a total inventory of 168 had to be repaired. Though the perceived distance between Sydney and South Africa is 6,200 miles, the yachts actually logged an average of 7,500 miles. "It was the ultimate test for the yachts and their crews" Roberts wrote. "No 'professional' crew could have worked harder at racing the yachts than the 'amateur' Challenge crews."

The strain on the skippers was immense. Even Mike Golding, enduring his third "wrong way" circumnavigation, had the vacant stare of a disaster victim when he berthed at

Cape Town's Waterfront complex. "I was scared all the time" he admitted. "I know better than the crew what can go wrong. The best thing about this trip is that it is the last time I'll go round this way. Definitely." Tom O'Connor, the relatively inexperienced sailor in charge of *Pause to Remember*, drew, to the point of utter exhaustion, on instincts for self-preservation he developed as a pilot of search-and-rescue helicopters in the Irish Air Corps. "You can feel every sheet of metal writhing in agony, every rivet vibrating" he told journalist Elaine Thompson, one of the fleet's most perceptive camp followers. "At times there

was no safety margin. This is the wildest ocean in the world. It's very unforgiving, and fourteen people's lives in my hands is a lot to bear."

O'Connor and Golding shared, with Hatfield, the searing memory of momentary fear that they had lost a man overboard. O'Connor leapt from the wheel in alarm to retrieve a crew member who, though wearing a lifeline, had been washed through the guardrail while attempting to free a fouled sheet on the leeward side of the boat. Golding was also at the helm, but helpless as one of a sail-folding party, who was not clipped on, was saved by the strength of a stanchion. Convention demanded that the victims remained anonymous. The logic of the long-distance racer insists such matters are kept in-house. The release of names would merely emphasize the suppressed sense of guilt at the inherent risks of the exercise. A yacht works on mutual trust, and on the fundamental principle that what the relatives don't know cannot harm them. It might go against my professional instincts, but, to this day, I have never revealed the identity of the person washed over *Hofbrau*'s bow on the previous race. I never will, because I suspect his wife still does not know.

Professional skippers, however, generate different rules of engagement. It was, therefore, soon a matter of public record that Paul Bennett, on *Ocean Rover*, was pulled to safety by his crew when he was washed over the side to the full extent of his lifeline. He had cause to cherish their prompt response to adversity, since being hauled at speed underwater, through an

ABOVE: THE MINIMUM NUMBER OF CREW ARE KEPT ON DECK ABOARD *GLOBAL TEAMWORK* AS THE WEATHER DETERIORATES.

RIGHT: REPAIRS BEING MADE TO THE *GLOBAL TEAMWORK* SPINNAKER POLE.

icy sea that offers a minimal prospect of long-term survival, is the stuff of nightmares. When it was all over, and he had begun to appreciate the comforts of Cape Town, he was to tell Thompson: "It was real Tommy-in-the-trenches stuff. Going up to do sail changes felt like going over the top. I've never ever had to dig so deep. We've all got a different perspective of what a problem is. Now, when a tax bill comes, or we lose a credit card, it will never seem the big thing it once was."

It was often unavoidable that the skippers should lead by unfortunate example. Merfyn Owen helmed his yacht, *Global Teamwork*, as it plunged furthest south from Tasmania. The immediate reward, of taking an early lead in the leg after a pleasant potter down the Australian coast, was ephemeral. The cost was obvious. He attempted to articulate his discomfort to an on-board video camera operated by Julia Bishop, but could not speak because his face, exposed to high-velocity, low-temperature winds, was numbed. From behind a partial yellow facemask, he burbled like a dentist's patient struggling to come around from a pain-killing injection into the jawline. "I can't talk" he said, speaking most effectively with his dark, wide eyes. "We've gone through every sail change in the book. What really interests me is why, and how, the crew bring themselves to go through this. My only hope is my nose doesn't drop off in the process."

On *Concert*, Chris Tibbs shared the solidarity of sacrifice. He was handicapped for several months after he, and three crew members, were swamped by a vicious wave which loomed from a breaking sea. He dislocated his shoulder, cracked his head on the pushpit of the boat, and sustained damage to the intricate semi-circular canals of his inner ear, which affected his natural sense of balance. He considered himself fortunate. His companions suffered either physically or, equally predictably, mentally. One broke his collarbone, another his hand, and a third was traumatized when he discovered his lifeline, the umbilical chord that linked him to his crew and boat, had been severed, as if by a cutlass.

Hugh Fogerty, Bennett's first mate on *Ocean Rover*, was moved to write : "I can now understand why people, in times of crisis, turn to the church. If anyone thought Hell was full of fire and damnation they were wrong. It is full of ice cold water and is situated below 53° south in the southern Indian Ocean." The human toll began to rise, relentlessly. Plastic surgeon Stewart Watson began the repair programme by stitching the index finger of *Courtaulds* crew member Carl Tinson, who had caught it in the mainsheet block. Steve Gooding, the most important member of *Motorola*'s foredeck crew, fell from the spinnaker pole and broke a collarbone. Skipper Mark Lodge, who admitted with a rueful smile that "I thought my days of being that far

FAR LEFT: THE POWER OF THE "WILDEST OCEAN IN THE WORLD" IS CLEARLY EVIDENT ON BOARD *COURTAULDS INTERNATIONAL*.

LEFT: ICE FORMING ON THE HELMSMAN GIVES AN IDEA OF THE WINDCHILL EFFECT WHICH CAUSED TEMPERATURES TO FEEL AS LOW AS MINUS 30° CENTIGRADE.

RIGHT: A TERRIFYING SEA AS SEEN FROM ON BOARD *SAVE THE CHILDREN*. HUGH FOGERTY ON *OCEAN ROVER* WROTE: "IF ANYONE THOUGHT HELL WAS FULL OF FIRE AND DAMNATION THEY WERE WRONG. IT IS FULL OF ICE COLD WATER AND IS SITUATED BELOW 53° SOUTH IN THE SOUTHERN INDIAN OCEAN".

forward on a yacht were over", reorganized the watch system so that he exposed himself fully to the vagaries of fate.

A sail change, in a storm, is a unique examination of character. Anyone who purports to enjoy the experience of hauling several hundredweight of wet sailcloth around a slippery, absurdly angled, deck should be linked to the nearest lie detector, or encased in the nearest straightjacket. People get hurt at the sharp end of a boat. They are impaled on steel stays, submerged by tons of sea water, or bounced off metal winches. "You always feel vulnerable in that area" reflected Concert's Brian Beaumont. "To get to the inner forestay to begin changing a sail, you have to go through what is a bit of no-man's land. You have to psyche yourself up to go up there, because there is always a chance you are going to be knocked down by a big wave. Once you're there you do things as quickly as possible. It's a matter of get the old sail down, get the new sail up, and get out. The longer you're there, the greater the chance you'll be washed down the deck."

Malcolm Thornley, on 3Com, was confined to his bunk for three weeks after sustaining severe bruising of the muscles down one side of his spine. "It's like a torture chamber" he reported. "The boat is flying off the waves, but I've just got to lie here until the pain eases." When it did, he was put on sail repair duty. "At times it has seemed like a prison sentence" he said. "All I've been doing is sewing mailbags." David Shanks, on

LEFT: CHECKING THE HEADSAILS AT NIGHT IN THE SOUTHERN OCEAN, IN THIS CASE ON *GROUP 4*, IS NOT FOR THE FAINT HEARTED.

BELOW LEFT: *TIME & TIDE'S* SKIPPER JAMES HATFIELD PUTTING TO GOOD USE HIS FORMER OCCUPATION AS A RESTAURANT OWNER.

RIGHT: STILL MOMENTS FOR FUN AS GRAHME RAYNER FROM *TIME & TIDE* FLAUNTS ONE OF HIS "SEALEGS".

BELOW: *SAVE THE CHILDREN'S* COMPASS GAVE UP THE GHOST – TOGETHER WITH THE REST OF HER INSTRUMENTS.

Commercial Union, spent a similar spell below deck when a huge wave forced the wheel into his stomach. He was helming at the time, and suffered sufficiently worrying abdominal injuries for fleet doctor Chris Price, on *Pause to Remember*, to sanction further consultation with the Haslar Hospital in Gosport. "There was an almighty crash" said *Commercial Union* colleague Alan Thomas, describing the incident. "I didn't know where I was, or which way the boat was up. Everything had been flung everywhere. The galley was a nightmare. You couldn't see the computer. It was covered in a mixture of white flower and potato mix, two inches deep."

If the elements were hard on man, they attempted to devastate machinery. The pump-action toilets on *Heath Insured II* and *Toshiba* exploded, with particularly gruesome results. *Courtaulds International*, whose skipper Webber admitted "we do not perform well in the deep latitudes of the Southern Ocean" made a drastic push northwards after suffering a knock-down that reduced three crew members to walking wounded. Life on *Save the Children* became barely tolerable in similar circumstances, which left Kevin Johnson nursing damaged ankle ligaments. Light bulbs began exploding without warning. Instruments gave bizarre readings before they expired completely. Crew members became prone to electric shocks when they touched bare metal. "A couple of hundred tons of water being dumped on you from a great height does you no favours" mused skipper Andy Hindley, whose job was complicated immeasurably when the boat's communication system failed. Without weather fax information, and reliable instrumentation, he was forced to sail blind. His only source of data was the six-hourly position report, and the barometric pressure. Faced with this, he canvassed his crew, and gambled a place among the pacemaking pack by heading north.

Pause to Remember were jostling for position in the middle of the fleet when they were overtaken by the calamity which served to emphasize their underdog mentality. Their boom suddenly snapped in two, an unthinkable handicap with 3,000 miles still to sail. The only option seemed to be to motor to the Kerguelen Islands, a former whaling colony developed as a scientific base by the French. O'Connor, who somehow produced a round of Irish coffees to lubricate the debate, successfully argued against abandoning the race. The boom, which weighed the equivalent of the average pack of rugby forwards, was wrestled below deck where, for seventy-two hours, Graham Philip, Matt Reeves and Ron Goddard devised and developed an ingenious repair. This involved making a metal sleeve with rudimentary tools, which was fitted over the alloy tube of the boom. A spinnaker pole was used as a splint, but fate chose to conspire against them. Within a matter of hours of the boom's reinstallation, the mainsail was torn asunder by winds which increased with frightening speed from twenty-five knots to seventy-five knots. Inevitably, cruelly, the British Legion boat joined *Courtaulds* and *Heath Insured II* among the also rans.

There were parallel compensations in the purity of the climate. Icebergs, in the throes of stately self-destruction, were the stuff of schoolboy fantasy. Nights, unpolluted by the reflected lights which signal civilization, were dark but clear. All that could be detected of humanity was the occasional satellite, moving slowly across the sky in an entrancing arc. It was impossible not to marvel at the Aurora Australis, the Southern Lights. The sky glowed green the instant before sunset. Even the storms had a terrible beauty. As the irrepressible Hatfield reported: "The sky all around us is constantly being lit up by flashes of millions of volts of electricity, which momentarily blind the helm. The rig is slack, the crew is whacked, the sheets are chafed and the sails are worn."

Gradually, in a competitive sense, the dice began to fall. *Save the Children*'s hike northwards had paid immediate dividends, but she was becalmed in an unseen high-pressure cell, and eventually finished sixth. Hindley, literally intoxicated by victory in Sydney, was beside himself as he coaxed the boat towards Cape Town in a maddeningly light breeze. "We've blown up everything electrical" he mourned, oblivious to the splendours of dawn breaking over the fairest Cape, at the southern tip of Africa. "The radio, the heaters, the instruments, the weather fax, the computers. The boat just went bananas. There you go. It's cost us this leg and probably the race."

Yet his disappointment paled into insignificance along-

FAR LEFT: *PAUSE TO REMEMBER'S* CREW MAN-HANDLING THEIR BROKEN BOOM. DESPITE AN INGENIOUS REPAIR, THE WEATHER INFLICTED YET MORE DAMAGE TO PUT THEM AMONG THE ALSO-RANS.

FAR LEFT, BOTTOM: A CLOSE-UP OF THE BROKEN BOOM SHOWING THE IMPROMPTU REPAIR WORK, THE SPINNAKER POLE ACTING AS A SPLINT.

LEFT: THEY CALL THE SEA OFF CAPE TOWN "THE PARKING LOT". HERE'S WHY.

BELOW: PAUL SHERWOOD, THE YOUNGEST CREWMAN IN THE RACE ENJOYS THE VIEW OF TABLE MOUNTAIN FROM *SAVE THE CHILDREN'S* SPINNAKER POLE.

LEFT: *GROUP 4* ARRIVE THROUGH THE LIFTING BRIDGE TO THEIR THIRD STAGE WIN OUT OF FOUR, JUST MOMENTS AHEAD OF *CONCERT*.

BELOW LEFT: *CONCERT*'S CHRIS TIBBS MASKS HIS BITTER DISAPPOINTMENT WHILE CONGRATULATING MIKE GOLDING.

RIGHT: *SAVE THE CHILDREN* GETTING A WARM RECEPTION.

BELOW RIGHT: *TOSHIBA WAVE WARRIOR*'S SKIPPER SIMON WALKER GREETING HIS YOUNG SON JACK.

BELOW: *GLOBAL TEAMWORK*'S CREW WERE FORCED TO ARRIVE AT THE DOCKSIDE BY WATER TAXI DUE TO A MECHANICAL FAILURE OF THE DOCK BRIDGE.

side that of Tibbs, who had taken the lead from *Group 4* as they closed on the coast. Golding gambled, by staying offshore, and re-established a four-mile advantage as the final afternoon wore on. They were eventually borne over the finishing line by the current. This unseen assistance offset the effect of the land breeze, which rolled off the mountains a matter of minutes too late for *Concert* to complete their unfinished business with the Southern Ocean. Tibbs, who had taken the decision to hug the coastline, broke down in tears. He had been beaten by nine-tenths of a mile, and thought momentarily of disqualifying himself by turning on the yacht's engine. "I can't believe it" he said. "To be beaten by that margin, after all those miles, is quite a bitter pill to swallow. We were watching them on the radar all the time. We were catching them up. . ." He stopped, as if unable or unwilling to prolong the agony of self-analysis. Golding, at least, had the decency to empathize. "I can't believe my luck" he conceded. "To win three legs is beyond my wildest fantasies."

Toshiba finished third, four hours later. Richard Merriweather brought *Commercial Union* in that evening, more than eight hours ahead of Lodge, on fifth-placed *Motorola*. *3Com* pipped *Global Teamwork* for seventh by thirty-five minutes, an achievement which prompted Jane Corfield to suggest "we all

RIGHT: Table Mountain looms over the Cape and the assembled yachts as the curious crowds come to look.

FAR RIGHT: *Heath Insured II* and a family reunion for the Pilkingtons.

FAR RIGHT, BOTTOM: The view atop *Ocean Rover* with the other yachts aligned underneath.

feel a little bit of a hero". *Time & Tide* were tenth, and Hatfield enthused to anyone who would listen about "my amazing guys". As he said: "They are awesome people, very humble and with nerves of steel". Tudor's disintegration was completed when he arrived ten hours later, a performance that dropped *Nuclear Electric* to ninth overall. The understated confidence of the pre-race favourite had disappeared. He swigged champagne from the bottle, but was close to despair. "I hated every minute of it" he said. "Every minute of it. My body, everything around and about me, hurts. My hands, my heart. I hate it. . ." Adrian Donovan, another veteran of the previous race, was equally distraught. He stayed below deck, when he finished last after being outmanouevred by O'Connor in the wind shadow cast by Table Mountain, to drown his sorrows.

But, in truth, there was nothing of which to be ashamed. The leaderboard of the BT Global Challenge is conspicuous not for what it contains, but for what it excludes. Just as no price can be put on the raw courage of the crews, no points system can do justice to the all-encompassing duties of a skipper. They must be men for all seasons, a cross between a diplomat, a doctor, a missionary and a mercenary. Each and every one of them looked gaunt when they arrived in Cape Town. Their eyes seemed somehow deeper set into faces pinched by tension. They needed a rest, a reprieve from their memories.

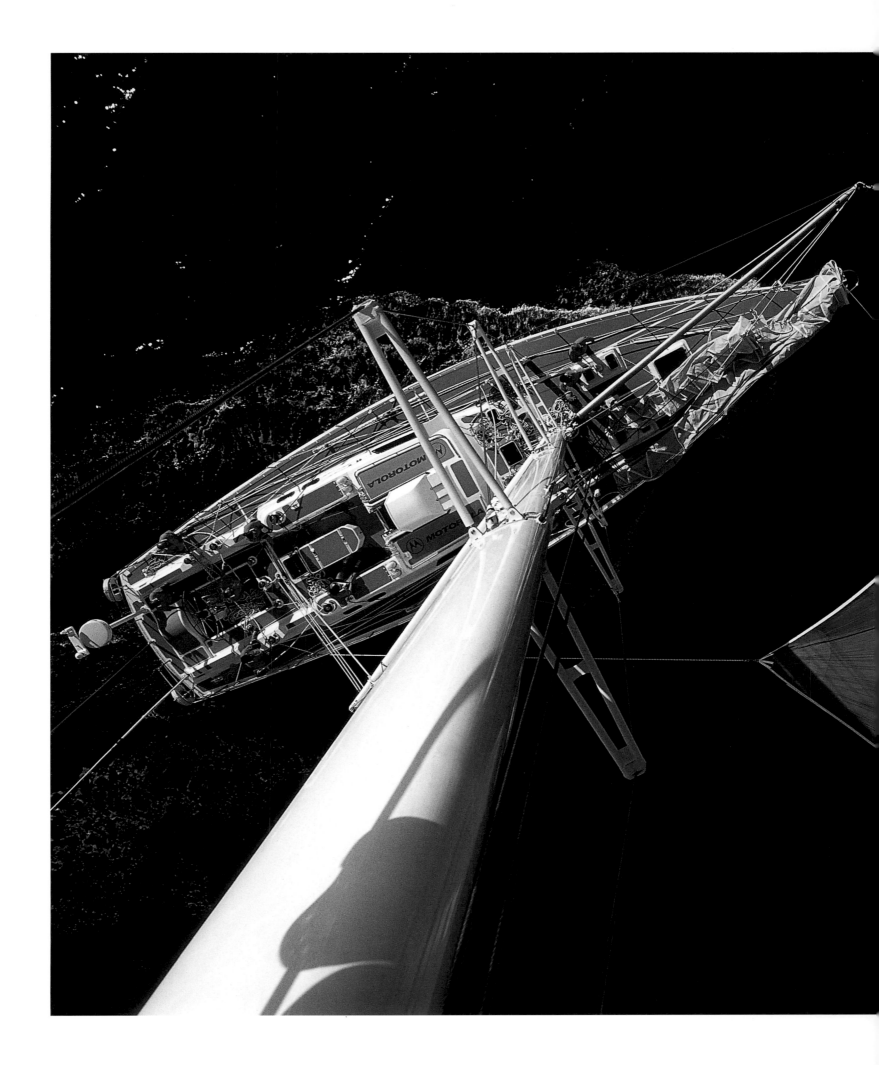

Go West

7,000 miles

The scions of Challenge chic took to wearing a specially designed tee shirt during the Cape Town stop over. "Southern Ocean" it read. "Been There. Done That. Never Going Back Again." A fashion statement, if ever there was one. Crews were more than happy to exchange the dangers of a rolling foredeck for the debauchery of the Rocking Shamrock, a particularly raucous Irish bar that became the epicentre of a social earthquake. Since dancing on the tables was obligatory, rather than merely permitted, it caught the prevailing mood. There was a palpable sense of relief. It was considered imperative that survival be celebrated. Many had already achieved a primary objective of a passage across the bottom of the world, which offered a matchless character reference.

LEFT: THE VIEW FROM THE TOP. YOU DO NOT FORGET THE SENSATION OF CLINGING TO THE MAST AS THE WIND FILLS THE SPINNAKER WHILE THE YACHT HEADS DOWNWIND. EACH YACHT CARRIED A NUMBER OF SPINNAKERS DESIGNED FOR DIFFERENT WIND STRENGTHS.

They had discovered that awe is sometimes more powerful than fear, that there is beauty in nature's beast. The surprising monotony of mountainous seas offered the sailors a unique reference point on dry land.

Boris Webber, skipper of *Courtaulds International*, and Kobus Kotze, a Cape Province farmer who sailed on *Toshiba Wave Warrior*, were duly celebrated as local boys made good. But the interest the fleet aroused was global. Messages of solidarity came from all points of the compass, from the Middle East to North America, West Africa to South America. A worldwide forum, set up on the BT internet site to offer strangers a chance to communicate with the yachts, revealed a notably reflective disposition. Merfyn Owen, *Global Teamwork*'s skipper, was sufficiently insulated from the privations of the Southern Ocean to tell a Kuwaiti schoolgirl: "It's clean and refreshing, a fantastic wilderness". Trevor Corner, from *Commercial Union*, shared "the extraordinary sight of a whale's tail in the moonlight, looming out of the sea only yards away from the boat". Tom O'Connor, skipper of *Pause to Remember*, summed up: "When you are thousands of miles away from civilization it is a strange feeling. You can get very close to nature, and experience wonderful unspoiled delights. The huge blue and green waves, the marine life. The weather constantly adds an unknown element to each day."

There was also still a race to be run, and won. The priority for *Group 4*, leading by a little under twenty-three hours from *Toshiba* with two legs of the race remaining, was to protect their advantage. If Mike Golding imposed his familiar disciplines on the 7,000-mile journey to Boston, they seemed vulnerable only to ill fortune, or a brave gamble by a skipper ready to rationalize the risk of doing something different. Step forward Mark Lodge, on *Motorola*. Considering overall fourth place expendable in emergency, he closeted himself away with John Crozier, one of his watch leaders, within seventy-two hours of their arrival in Cape Town. He lacked the professional guidance expensively acquired by such skippers as Golding and Owen, but as he pored over weather data Lodge was prepared to back his instincts. The plan, unveiled secretly to the crew five days before the restart, was to steal away from the fleet. Heading west immediately would condemn them to last place, but carried the promise of long-term reward. Lodge knew that above all else, the race hinged on the renegotiation of the Doldrums, and the

avoidance of the infamous Azores High. A boat in the right place at the right time could make up as much as four days on the rest.

Of course, there were doubts. Lodge faced a definitive examination of his leadership qualities. He scanned his crew minutely as he outlined his strategy, and recognized the doubters. "It's a big gamble" he told them, with characteristic bluntness. "But it's really an easy choice. I've known for six months that this is the time for us to make our move. This is the only leg in which there is a chance to make big gains. It's too easy to follow the rest. We have to totally disregard them, do our own thing. It will get twitchy. You're going to see yourself going down the leaderboard. The people at home, who don't know what we're doing, will see us go from tenth, to twelfth, to four-teenth, and wonder what on earth is going on. We've got to have confidence in the boat, and the people on it. I know I have."

Consequently, as his crew wound in the winches during the pre-start jousting, Lodge bellowed a simple entreaty. "Go on. Want it." It was an emotional response to the competitive stresses of a day which unfolded as a mixture of solemnity and celebration. Archbishop Desmond Tutu, impressed by the open boat policy that had welcomed disadvantaged groups of town-ship children, began by blessing the fleet. Crews said their farewells in a scrum of minstrels, mime artists and jazz musi-cians. Webber, acutely aware of live coverage on South African television, responded to the occasion with the aggression of a natural racer, crossing the line first, ahead of *3Com* and *Nuclear Electric*. *Heath Insured II* had taken the lead by the second mark, but it was to be a brief burst of exhilaration. Chay Blyth might have characterized this penultimate leg as "being all sun-

shine, mermaids and gin and tonics" but its strains were subtle, insidious. The crews were preparing to tiptoe through a meteorological minefield. Subconsciously at least, they had found the brutality of the Southern Ocean comforting. Hardship somehow becomes acceptable through familiarity and the frustrations of sailing through light airs, coaxing the last percentage point out of unsuitably heavy steel yachts, took their toll.

Sail damage, primarily to the spinnakers, signalled impatience. Sleep remained elusive. The heat exaggerated latent tensions, brought relationships to the boil. A minor dispute, such as the timing of breakfast on *Heath*, led to a fist fight. Two feuding crewmates had to be separated on *Ocean Rover*. This was not in itself unusual. A precedent had been set on *3Com* earlier in the race when a punch was thrown at mate Kieron O'Connell. More worrying was the subsequent struggle of *Rover* skipper Paul Bennett to retain respect. He was a victim of the event's central inconsistency. Some crew members felt his inability to race the boat hard had bred a defeatist attitude. In the words of Jon Hirsh "we must get out of the feeling that other boats are better than us". The contrary view criticized Bennett for ignoring the philosophical significance of the event. Competitiveness was considered an occupational hazard of circumnavigating the globe.

LEFT, TOP: THE YACHTS TUSSLE WITH FLUKEY WINDS IN TABLE BAY.

LEFT, BOTTOM: *CONCERT* UNDER SPINNAKER.

RIGHT: THE SCENE ON THE FOREDECK OF *NUCLEAR ELECTRIC*.

"It was very very difficult" Bennett acknowledged. "It was too hot, too unforgiving. It just got to people. For the first time, tempers flew. The majority wanted to race, but four or five of them would be quite happy to sit at the back of the boat with a gin and tonic and just get around. I can understand that mentality, because I've dealt with it before, but the extremely keen sailors in the crew find it frustrating. The problem had been pushed aside in the Southern Ocean, simply because it is so daunting. That was just about survival. We're all adults, but when you are at sea with nothing to do but think all day you can become quite childish. I don't like any form of argument, but in

retrospect, it had to happen. This has been a huge event. My guys were beginning to think of having to rehabilitate themselves, to get back to whatever normality represents. Some of them are going to struggle."

The conflict was duplicated on *Pause to Remember*. Julian Davis has long term ambitions in long-distance sailing, and was exasperated that he became conspicuous for his commitment. "It was hard for the skipper to motivate anyone when things kept going wrong" he admitted. "People switched off. They want to move on, get home. I want to carry on racing, but they're quite happy to cruise." Blyth was unrepentant. "You will

RIGHT: *OCEAN ROVER*, UNDER SPINNAKER AT THE START, CATCHES A WAVE AGAINST THE MAJESTIC SETTING OF THE CAPE AND TABLE MOUNTAIN.

always get that conflict" he argued. "You'll get people who want adventure, a challenge. Equally, you'll also get people who want to get very 'yottie', and race like Hell around the world. We try to alleviate the problem during training, but once you hand the crews over to the skippers they develop their own culture."

Dr Alan Rudge, deputy chief executive of BT, drew on his direct experience of the emotions engendered by isolation. He sailed on *Global Teamwork* in the third leg, and was to transfer to the yacht *Concert* for the final transatlantic sprint to Southampton. He had an alternative agenda, a different perspective. He involved the company in the project because it represented a multi-faceted business opportunity, but recognized it would also provide the perfect managerial case study. Incongruously, the disputes justified his foresight. "All the pressures of life are brought into a sharp focus on a yacht" he explained. "The Challenge is a different race to any other. You take a cross-section of people, of all ages, abilities, sizes and sexes, and place them in an intense environment. They live on top of each other in miserable circumstances. Management is the key. Skippers must deal with the responsibility of what can be life or death situations. They must develop the right atmosphere. They must motivate their crew to complete sail change after sail change in dirty weather. A successful boat is a meritocracy, which encourages teamwork. There is a lot to be learned by any senior manager who wants to be observant."

To borrow from a famous tabloid masthead, all human life is, indeed, there. Almost inevitably, there were temper tantrums on *Time & Tide*, where the stress of fractured personal relationships began to manifest itself. One dissident abandoned the wheel, when the boat was surfing downwind under spinnaker. Another simply refused to work. Subsequent criti-

cism of the autocratic style of skipper James Hatfield was manifestly unfair, given the range of physical and mental frailty to which he was obliged to respond. His disabled sailors were simply not strong enough to cope with the required frequency of sail changes in gentle winds and, as they began to lose contact at the back of the fleet, morale dropped. Without firm leadership a boat containing such diverse, uniquely driven individuals would have foundered. As Hatfield had always suspected, he

ABOVE: SORTING OUT THE JUMBLE OF SHEETS ON BOARD *PAUSE TO REMEMBER*. THE COLOURS HELP TO EASE THE CONFUSION.

LEFT: ACROBATICS ON *COURTAULDS INTERNATIONAL*, STAGED FROM THE END OF THE SPINNAKER POLE.

RIGHT: AN UNUSUAL VIEW OF THE *SAVE THE CHILDREN* SPINNAKER WITH A CREWMAN AT THE TOP.

FAR RIGHT: BELOW DECKS ON *TIME & TIDE*.

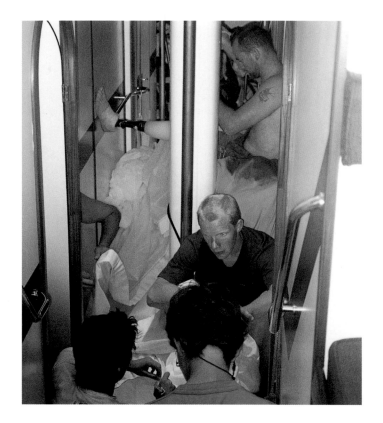

was eventually forced to accentuate weaknesses. This left mental scars, as vivid as the slashes which signalled his sustained heart surgery. He refused blithely to ignore the consequences of his actions, and readily offered an insight into a troubled conscience. There was an affecting wistfulness in his reflection that "because there's no visual display of pain it's hard to know what's going on inside, and what to do about it. It was horrible because it made a lot of people question what they had to go home to."

The future began to loom large as the boats began to park in mid-Atlantic. Minds wandered to abandoned jobs and families. For the first time in months, such apparently alien notions as personal security and domestic harmony seemed a priority. The ritual of sitting on the rail, and staring out onto a flat sea as the wind-starved mainsail panted for breath, was cathartic. Some, like *Motorola*'s Mark Baptist, welcomed the change in circumstance. "From being a damage limitation exercise, yacht racing has become a pleasurable experience once again" he reported. Unsurprisingly, he found an ally in his girlfriend, *Toshiba*'s Jo Watson. Clearly moved by the moment, she was positively poetic, observing: "Stunning sunsets abound, reflecting flame orange rays as the equatorial sun dips below the horizon once again. We stare heavenwards, admiring misty moon halos and attempting to name the stars and constellations, which are ever-changing as we voyage around the world."

Others were not so convinced, so poetic. The images summoned by *Save the Children*'s Paul Sherwood, the youngest crewman in the race, were markedly more doom-laden. "The

spinnaker hangs in the rigging like a convicted man from the gallows" he reported to race HQ, as the boat sat in an airless void. The mood on *Courtaulds International* was hardly helped when they were overtaken by a plastic lawn chair, floating in an oily sea populated by Portuguese Man O'War jellyfish. *Nuclear Electric*'s Simon Montague suggested "this has become far too sedate. Some of us are wishing for a full Southern Ocean gale to spice things up a bit". On *Concert*, skipper Chris Tibbs sensed complacency setting in and asked: "Isn't it all too easy? Was the cold and wet really that bad?" Only the ironic wit of the imperturbable Hatfield was unaffected. "I now realize the world is flat and not round" he wrote. "I can confirm we have fallen over the edge. How much worse can things get?"

Worse, much worse. Even elation was illusory. Richard Merriweather's crew on *Commercial Union*, profiting from their position on the northern fringe of the fleet, took the lead. "The emotion that ran through the boat was incredible" remembered Tim Burrows. "Everyone was on an absolute high. The effort they were prepared to put in was phenomenal." Yet, within days, they were becalmed. Boats sailed up to and around them, as if borne on a private wind. For Merriweather, who had

been reduced to smoking tea to ward off his craving for nicotine, it was too, too, much. The subsequent crossing of their outward path, which provided technical confirmation that they had sailed around the world, was a crushing anti-climax.

Priorities change, but principles must endure. So when *Heath* were alerted to an apparently untended yacht, drifting aimlessly in the middle of nowhere, they investigated out of a strange sense of curiosity and duty. It was an eerie sight in the early morning light, apparently summoned from schoolboy fantasies of the *Marie Celeste*, but ultimately deceptive. The yacht was, in fact, fully crewed. They were fast asleep below deck, oblivious to the alarm they had created. *Heath* skipper Adrian Donovan accepted their bashful apologies, and soon had another more tangible problem to consider. The Curse of Andy Pilkington was about to strike with fateful consequences.

Pilkington, who sold his garage business in Chorley, Lancashire, to finance his involvement, had emerged as a diligent, naturally talented sailor. His instinct for adventure, given full rein by cave diving, canoeing and a trans-African motorcycle journey, was self-evident. Yet he was unlucky. He sustained a head injury during the inter-fleet Fastnet race, and cracked his ribs on the first Southern Ocean leg to Wellington. An hour after coming off a routine foredeck watch, two weeks north of Cape Town, his ambition to sail around the world was destroyed. His pulse raced and his temperature soared. He was in such agonizing stomach pain that Donovan felt he had no alternative but to switch on *Heath*'s engine, and make a 170-mile diversion to St Helena, the volcanic outcrop in the South Atlantic that gained global notoriety when it was chosen by the

British as the site for Napoleon's exile, and death. Pilkington was heavily drugged thirty-six hours later, when he was ferried into a flat-bottomed boat, which took him through a deceptively difficult swell. He retains a searing image of looking up at the island's mile-high cliffs. At that moment, he felt as desolate as the setting.

"I was very emotional" he recalled. "It's probably the first time that something has brought tears to my eyes. I'd never considered that illness would prevent me doing the whole trip and suddenly, I was struck by a sense of underachievement. I wasn't going to sail around the world. I felt I was letting the crew down, and I swore blind that I would never set foot on a yacht again. There were so many conflicting things going on in my mind. I was pretty doped up, but I was in such pain that if you had given me the option of being beamed to the moon to recover I'd have accepted. I felt like I'd been hit with a sledgehammer. There were times when I even considered the thought that I was dying. Yet, when I was being taken off the yacht all I could see was this dark dismal rock in the middle of the South Atlantic. I was devastated. Even before *Heath* had sailed away, I began missing the yacht, and everyone on it, very badly."

The initial diagnosis, of acute appendicitis, was contradicted in the island's only hospital. Local doctors detected that Pilkington was merely passing kidney stones, and he was given a clean bill of health within five days. Regrettably, repatriation was not that simple. It took a fortnight for the mail ship HMS *St Helena* to transport him to Ascension Island, where, after a ticketless hiatus spent swimming with giant turtles, he took an RAF Hercules to Brize Norton, Oxfordshire. He spent five days with his family before he flew to Boston to await his crew and his wife Carol, who had signed up to sail the final leg on *3Com*. The promises of disaffection with yachting, made in the heat of the moment, were as worthless as a confidence trickster's promise.

So, too, were many cherished gameplans. *Commercial Union* might have been first to cross the Equator but like *Toshiba*, who had taken a more easterly route, they were quickly consumed by the Azores High. Losses of up to 250 miles in forty-eight hours were frequent. On *Courtaulds*, who rose from eighth to third as they ghosted through the parking lot of the Sargasso Sea, Suse Goulder discovered "one of the unspoken truths of the Challenge". She observed: "No one tells you this beforehand, but the long sunny days are just as bad as a tough one in the Southern Ocean." The most conspicuous advance was made by *Motorola* on the western edge of the fleet. Lodge's hunch was correct. The perseverance of his crew was rewarded as they sailed around their struggling rivals. They lacked wind instruments but were, on average, two knots faster. The six-hourly position reports could not come quickly enough. Morale was high. Life was good. But victory was out of the question. There were no prizes for guessing the identity of the solitary yacht they could not catch. Golding, a professional

ALL: CRISIS, WHAT CRISIS?
ANOTHER SELECTION OF PICTURES
DEPICTING VARIED ANTICS AS THE
VESSELS RECROSS THE EQUATOR.
ANYTHING TO EASE THE TENSION.

LEFT: *TOSHIBA WAVE WARRIOR* ARRIVING IN BOSTON IN THIRD PLACE.

BELOW: THE SEABIRDS AND THE SUNSET GREET *COURTAULDS INTERNATIONAL* AS SHE ARRIVES IN FOURTH POSITION.

to the core, feared and respected Lodge's ploy, but had kept just enough in reserve to claim his fourth win in five legs.

Blyth denied the dominance of *Group 4* had killed the Challenge as a competitive entity, arguing: "whichever way you look at it, what they've done is a phenomenal achievement." But as they entered Boston Harbor, Golding's crew were in the unfair position of having almost to justify their excellence. There was something mundane in the triumphant images of champagne showers and trophy presentations. As the former fireman was compelled to outline his principles, he was in the risible position of a politician apologizing for a landslide majority. "The number one thing is that everyone on the boat gets on" he said. "If there is any problem within the crew it is picked up quickly, and dealt with. People don't realize the tremendous

amount of work the crew do. They've given up potentially free time in the ports of call to prepare the boat. We push hard and as we've become more successful we've pushed harder. That's the only way to work. Anyone with a competitive nature feels the need to prove himself, and I'm no different to the rest."

PR platitudes sneered the cynics. They whispered sourly about the regimentation of Golding's system, which utilized specialists in key positions at the bow and on the helm. They depicted commonsense as a cardinal sin, and accused him of betraying the Challenge ethos. Significantly, the counter-argument was led by Lodge when he arrived, to a tumultuous welcome sixteen hours later. "You can't run a race on ethos" he told Elaine Thompson. "Mike hasn't put a foot wrong." Golding was, understandably enough, irked by the crit-

icism. "The snipers say our approach is more professional than the rest" he reflected. "Well, I've always thought that is a bit of a strange word. Professionalism just means doing your job that little bit better. It's not really a criticism, it's a compliment. As the race has developed these crews have learned more and more. We are pushing the boats to the limit. You have only to look at the amount of rig damage incurred to see that. There were times in the Southern Ocean when we were out of control. I was sitting at the chart table with my knuckles going white, because I knew if the wind gained another knot we'd be in trouble. But, if I'm honest, part of the buzz of what we do is taking things to the very edge without losing the plot. The race has changed. It has lost its innocence. The camaraderie is there, but it only emerges when we're out at sea and push comes to shove. Then we realize we've only got each other to rely on."

Simon Walker, Golding's closest rival for overall victory, came in third, thirty hours behind the leader. He accepted the conventional wisdom that only a disaster of unforeseen proportions would allow him to make up his fifty-three hour deficit over the final leg. *Motorola* had taken overall third place from *Save the Children*, whose skipper Andy Hindley was on the verge of tears when he docked at Rowes Wharf. "It's been a struggle for me to keep them going" he confirmed in a low voice, which crackled with suppressed emotion. "Really, really hard." The *Commercial Union* crew, who finished a place further back, in seventh, were similarly crestfallen. "That was the

hardest leg of all" reported Bransom Bean. "The Southern Ocean has nothing to compare to the disappointment we feel right now."

There was a detectable shift in emphasis. For all their studied indifference to the public perception of suffering in the Southern Ocean, the crews felt good about themselves when they arrived in Cape Town. Now, a continent away in Boston, they had a strange compulsion to look on the dark side. The type of guilt felt by Simon Wardle, when he docked on *Nuclear*

Electric, was a mitigating factor. He had just caught a bottle of champagne, thrown by Blyth, when he noticed his wife Adele, holding their two-year-old daughter Alice on the pontoon. "My eyes popped out of my head" he admitted. Reunited for the first time in nine months, the family began to ease him away from the self-imposed restrictions of the Challenge. "It's been as hard for the families as it has been for us" he found himself reflecting. His wife did not disagree. "It's been torture" she said. "I can't wait till it is all over."

ABOVE LEFT: *GROUP 4* PRESENTED WITH YET ANOTHER COURTAULDS TROPHY AS LEG WINNERS, FOURTH TIME OUT OF FIVE.

LEFT: A TOAST TO *NUCLEAR ELECTRIC'S* ARRIVAL.

ABOVE: THE CREW OF *NUCLEAR ELECTRIC* GREET *TIME & TIDE*, LAST TO ARRIVE ON THIS LEG.

RIGHT: A WELCOME CASE OF THE LOCAL BEER IS TO HAND AS *TIME & TIDE* CREW PLAY THE LOCAL MEDIA GAME.

The Homecoming

3,000 miles

James Capstick gazed out of the window of the airbus ferrying him from Boston's Logan International Airport. The BT Global Challenge fleet, arranged neatly in the bay below, had the apparent vulnerability of matchstick boats, glued together by a shortsighted schoolboy. They seemed to belong to another radically different world. A world that he had fallen out of love with. As the jet banked away, at the start of its transatlantic journey, he promised himself he would never return to the yacht *Ocean Rover*. He would never again endure the pettiness of strangers subjected to each other's company. His alienation had been completed by the five-week journey from Cape Town. He was tired of making a conscious attempt to control his anger.

LEFT: *NUCLEAR ELECTRIC, MOTOROLA* AND *GROUP 4* ASSEMBLED ON THE BOSTON WATERFRONT PRIOR TO THE SIXTH AND FINAL LEG BACK TO SOUTHAMPTON. FOR THE CREWS A RETURN TO DOMESTIC, POSSIBLY MUNDANE, LIFE AND NORMALITY SUDDENLY LOOMED BEFORE THEM.

Tolerance was never a natural strength and, anyway, he had a family to repay. He had a career as a mounted policeman in London to resume. As far as he was concerned, the penultimate leg of the race was a leg too far.

Tracey Capstick was unaware of her husband's abrupt departure, little more than twenty-four hours after *Ocean Rover* became the twelfth Challenge boat to dock at Rowes Wharf. He had surmised, correctly, that her first instinct would have been to cancel the credit card which financed his flight back to their Surrey home. Her perspective had changed in the previous nine months. Her life revolved, more intimately than ever, around her children Stephen, Christopher and Georgia, the baby daughter born when her father was at sea. Tracey recognized the extent of his sacrifices, but could not forget her own concessions. She allowed him forty-eight hours grace, to wallow in self-pity. "Then she told me my fortune in no uncertain terms" James admitted. "The general theme was 'if you think you're going to back out now, after all the sacrifices we have made over the past four years, you've got another think coming'. Needless to say, ten days later I was on another plane, back to Boston, ready to race to Southampton and finish the Challenge."

His was not the only soul being searched. A dual cause for collective celebration, Mark Lodge's marriage to Michelle Lane, and the announcement of Chay Blyth's knighthood, signally failed to lift an air of apprehension. A transatlantic crossing meant nothing to amateur sailors with 30,000 competitive miles in their Royal Yachting Association (RYA) logbooks, but

the last leg had a disturbing finality. The prospect of domesticity hung heavily. It made many realize just how detached they had become. They were returning to a lost world, in which earnest dinner party guests discussed Tony Blair and the Teletubbies, the furry blobs who entranced the under-threes on Children's BBC. Only two of the crew of *Nuclear Electric*, for example, had heard of the Spice Girls, those platform-soled symbols of modernity. The only Girl Power they recognized was Jos Walters helping to haul Haken Rodebjer up the mast for a final pre-race rig check. As Simon Montague, who was contemplating a new job as BBC Transport Correspondent, observed: "The race has been a cocoon in which there are no vital deadlines or important decisions. The prospect of once again producing coherent thought and action is alarming."

Skippers, most notably those who had experienced the post-Challenge blues four years earlier, warned their crews of the impending ambush of anti-climax. Andy Hindley, on *Save the Children*, reflected: "I realized what I was letting myself in for at the start of all this. It doesn't make it any easier to deal with, and I've told my crew over and over again how difficult it will be for them to come down at the end of the race. They've

ABOVE RIGHT: SKIPPER JAMES HATFIELD GIVES A FINAL CREW BRIEFING TO HIS *TIME & TIDE* TEAM.

RIGHT *GROUP 4* ALREADY HAD THE RACE ALL BUT WON BY THE END OF LEG FIVE, LEADING *TOSHIBA* BY TWO DAYS.

FAR RIGHT: *3COM* RUNNING CLOSE TO *NUCLEAR ELECTRIC* BEFORE THE START. *3COM* WENT ON TO TAKE AN EARLY LEAD IN THE LEG.

got to have something else to focus on." Sean Blowers had that luxury but, once it became clear that back injuries would prevent him rejoining the *Commercial Union* crew as planned, it represented precious little consolation. His problems were an ominous indication of the transient nature of the society the BT Global Challenge racers were gearing themselves to rejoin. In short, he had been left to wonder whether he had sailed past his sell-by date.

Blowers, a warm, open-faced man, is a character in a profession that produces caricatures. An actor with a refreshing disregard for the egocentric conventions of Luvviedom, he had taken the gamble of having himself written out of *London's Burning*, the hugely popular TV series in which he starred, to compete in the race. He developed into one of its pivotal personalities. He worked hard on the boat, and played equally hard in port, a pre-requisite since his crew were the party animals of the fleet. Yet his enforced retirement from the Challenge in Wellington highlighted the rigours of rehabilitation. Parts he had been promised failed to materialize. Kick-starting his career had all the inherent difficulties of kick-starting a dubious MOT failure.

As he waited in Southampton for the boats to return, he wore his crew clothing almost as a token of respect. He radiated a poignant sense of personal loss. "I'm having to come to terms with those horrible things, like bills, mortgages and careers" he said, with revealingly enforced jollity. "However bad it is at sea, it is still easier than what we call normality. There is nothing else to think about but sailing the boat as fast as possible when you are out there. I was hoping to rejoin the crew, but did too much damage to my back. Recovering from that blow is all part of the challenge. You've just got to keep a grip on things."

Conversely, it was a time to appreciate retrospective achievements. Boris Webber's crew on *Courtaulds International* took time to gel, but once the human chemistry had stabilized, they shared an educational experience. They learned about collective loyalty when they rallied around Howard Metcalfe, who was an emotional casualty of the Southern Ocean and withdrew from the crew in New Zealand. They refined the art of compromise, in coming to terms with initial differences with their skipper. Mike Leadbetter came extremely close to emulating David Greaves, and resigning halfway through the race, but persevered. As he told Tim Jeffery, one of a number of journalists involved in a PR-conscious campaign, "people have made the necessary adjustments. I've tried very hard to keep my lip buttoned and Boris's approach to management has changed. I'm really pleased that I stuck in here."

Given the subdued surroundings, there was something appropriate about the sea-fog which shrouded the fleet as it

RIGHT: CONCENTRATE. *COURTAULDS INTERNATIONAL* AND *COMMERCIAL UNION* COAXING SPEED OUT OF THEIR SPINNAKERS AT THE BEGINNING OF THE LEG.

struggled in light winds four days out of Boston. The start had been brisk, enlivened by flukey winds from the city, but ultimately unexceptional. *Global Teamwork* led at the line, and *3Com* were first around the Alpha Waypoint. Climatic conditions lent a suitable air of mystery to proceedings which, once the mists lifted, developed with all the predictability of a heavy metal band's three-chord chorus. As usual, Mike Golding on *Group 4* took stock of the situation before he took an unassailable lead. Another leg win, the final gesture of superiority, was the climax of a flawless competitive campaign. Golding's crew were denied the acclamation of a daylight docking in Ocean Village, yet were somehow suited to the fleeting shadows of the early hours of 16 July 1997.

They were initially visible in the Solent as silhouettes, outlined against a mainsail illuminated by the spotlight of an attendant motor boat. Their body language had an ease of delivery which suggested they were rightly proud of their accomplishments, but there were no imposing personalities on board. The differences in character embodied by teammates like the scholarly Jack Ward and the streetwise Martin Hall were disguised. They were dressed identically, in hooped shirts

LEFT, TOP: ONE FOR THE SCRAPBOOK. THE *TOSHIBA* CREW POSE FOR THE CAMERA IN MID-ATLANTIC.

LEFT: EVERY PICTURE TELLS A STORY. *GROUP 4* AND *TOSHIBA*, FIRST AND SECOND OVERALL, ON THE FINAL LEG.

RIGHT: *GROUP 4* TRAILING TOSHIBA BEFORE THEY RE-ESTABLISHED THEIR SUPERIORITY OVER THE REST OF THE FLEET.

which were eventually offset by silk soccer-style rosettes which went out of fashion with wooden rattles. Each person appeared to be a cog, of varying size and shape, in a well-oiled wheel. There were indications of individualism, underlined by the social conscience of Andrea Bacon, who had been repelled by the materialism of her previous life in public relations, but the corporate connotations of success were unavoidable.

Understandably, the Group 4 employees on board appreciated the career path, cleared by success. The crew were

deemed to be favoured sons and daughters of sponsor Jorgen Philip Sorensen. This gave the critics an easy target, yet told a fraction of the real story. Appearances, remember, are notoriously deceptive. *Group 4* won because the diligence and determination of Golding was matched by the distinctive passion of his mentor, Sorensen. He might have the accoutrements and attitudes of massive personal wealth, but, like Blyth, he is best judged by his background. He has never forgotten his formative years as a penurious immigrant from Scandinavia. He lodged in

LEFT: Conditions nearing the end of the leg were very light. *Global Teamwork* and *Pause to Remember* try to catch what breeze there is.

ABOVE RIGHT: Skipper Richard Merriweather (left), master of the *Commercial Union* pipe band, with crew member Lars Hultgren.

RIGHT: Never a quiet moment at sea; there is always work to be done.

the back bedroom of a council house and worked on the night shift as a security guard. He depicts England as "the best country in the world" simply because it remains, in his view, one of the last meritocracies the world dares to permit. The BT Global Challenge fitted the same criteria.

"We are experiencing something rather unique" he said, as the company yacht surged along Southampton Water. He had a glass of champagne in his right hand and a torpedo of a Havana cigar in his left, but, spiritually, he was savouring bread and water. "I feel privileged to have been drawn into something like this. We're watching the cream of youth, proving themselves. I feel so good for them, for their skipper, and for the race that gave them their opportunity. I can't think of anyone who has influenced so many people's lives, on a basic level, as Chay Blyth. This, for me, is the experience of a lifetime. I feel relieved that they have come home safely, without mishaps. I would not trade this for anything." With that, he pushed his baseball cap to the back of his forehead, and wiped his eyes. The trademark tears were no theatrical ploy. Golding's previous crew, from the British Steel Challenge, were one deck below Sorensen on the support ship, but equally animated. As they wasted Epernay's finest in a spray that soared into the darkness they, too, felt they belonged. Don Deakin, for good measure, was congratulating himself on a winning bet that his successors would win five legs of the BT Global Challenge.

Fireworks were released to welcome the winners at 2.06 am BST, a gesture that provoked angry exchanges on local radio once the sun had come up. But, again, it was strangely appropriate that the time servers of suburbia should be woken by spectacular recognition of a different way of life. Golding's crew were glassy-eyed, almost shocked by the realization that it was all over. "This is the ultimate, the pinnacle of everything I've ever done" summed up Grahame Gibson, a key Group 4 executive who had flourished at sea. "It is the first time that what we have achieved has really sunk in. I am sure it has changed me. You go through tremendous highs and lows, for month after month. You learn so much about yourself. I'm different to the person who left here last September. Out there, I've come to terms with my weaknesses. Everyone has them and I can now manage mine. My strengths have become stronger. I can approach the future with such confidence."

Such optimism has the depth of vision defined by unlimited champagne, guzzled after weeks on a diet of freeze-dried cardboard. Yet, in Simon Walker's case, it seemed justified. He reinforced his status by steering his yacht *Toshiba Wave Warrior* to second place, overall and on the final leg. He managed to match magnanimity – "It would have been a travesty had anyone other than *Group 4* won" – with sensitivity. Not for the first time, he appreciated the importance of his wife Louise, and his two infant children. "Sailing is my life, what I want to do, but the pressures are immense" he said. "This race is as emotional for a skipper as it is for anyone. I missed my family.

I missed my two kids. That is a biological function. On a couple of the long legs I've sat on my own and wished I was not there." His wife, cradling their baby son in the cockpit, concurred. "The last ten months have gone very slowly" she said. "This is as much a challenge for the families as it is for the crews. They just manage to juggle."

So, in an entirely different manner, did Alan Rudge. He took holiday leave to sail from Boston on *Concert* but sluggish winds threatened his attendance at BT's annual general meeting, on the morning of 16 July. His original intention, to be air-lifted off the boat in the interests of corporate harmony, was scuppered by the race committee, who threatened to disqualify the yacht on the grounds of outside interference. From that moment on it became, in his words, "a case of get me to the church on time." Chris Tibbs, *Concert*'s skipper, was 1,000 miles out of Ocean Village when he decreed that the finishing line had to be reached by 5am on the appointed day. He was late, as it turned out. A whole seven minutes late. Rudge's transport policy, which involved him being transferred from inflatable rib to chauffeured car and private aeroplane, was so precise that he arrived in Edinburgh for the annual meeting, half an hour early. A querulous shareholder, evidently primed to embarrass the board, began the meeting by asking "where is Dr Rudge?" "Here" came the answer, amplified by an outstretched arm. "No further questions" said the would-be rabble rouser.

FAR LEFT: TEN MONTHS AND 29,000 MILES LATER A VICTORIOUS *GROUP 4* CREW ARRIVE BACK IN SOUTHAMPTON JUST AFTER 2AM LOCAL TIME.

LEFT, TOP TO BOTTOM: THE EARLY BATH. THE *GROUP 4* CREW CELEBRATE THEIR WIN BY DUCKING SKIPPER MIKE GOLDING.

LEFT: LONG A WELCOMING SIGHT TO HOMECOMING BRITISH MARINERS, THE NEEDLES OFF THE ISLE OF WIGHT.

By this time, *Save the Children* and *Commercial Union* were converging on the Solent. They traded tack for tack before Hindley, who had celebrated his thirtieth birthday the previous day, confirmed overall third place by crossing the finishing line ninety-six seconds ahead. Then, and only then, could the crews appreciate the occasion. Crowds, five deep, lined the walkways. Relatives waited on the pontoon. As soon as *Save the Children* docked, Philip White was swamped by the tearful embrace of his wife and two daughters. He had not dared to return to them from New Zealand, as planned, because he doubted his capacity to rejoin the boat. "It's all been worth it" he concluded.

"Chay used to tell us: 'No Guts, No Glory'. Well, I'm glad I had the guts to do this, and grateful for the glory it has given me." There were similar scenes when *Commercial Union* tied up for the last time. Nick Auger, swinging from the forestay, waved frantically at his four daughters, who had "Welcome Home Daddy" painted in blue letters on their foreheads. "Thank goodness I'm wearing these" he said, pushing back his sunglasses with his index finger. "At least you won't see me crying. It's been absolutely incredible. I've gone through so much, learned so much about myself. I feel refreshed. This is the start of a new life."

ABOVE: *COMMERCIAL UNION*
JOUSTED WITH *SAVE THE CHILDREN*
FOR THE HONOUR OF FINISHING
FOURTH ON THE LEG, BUT LOST.

LEFT AND RIGHT: JUST SECONDS
AHEAD OF *COMMERCIAL·UNION*
(CLEARLY VISIBLE IN THE
BACKGROUND), *SAVE THE CHILDREN*
ACHIEVED THIRD PLACE OVERALL.

Nine yachts finished within an hour that evening. Five
crossed the line within nine minutes. Improbably, after 3,000
miles, *3Com* beat *Courtaulds International* by three seconds.
The welcome was uniformly ecstatic but, in the chaos of celebration, it was possible to detect cameos of real intimacy. Peter
Calvin stood in the cockpit of *Nuclear Electric* and held his son
Jack, born on the eve of the race, to his cheek. "It will be so good
to see much more of him" he said. James Capstick made the
laddish gesture of wearing a viking's helmet, which identified
him as an *Ocean Rover* crew member, but he, too, was ready to
be a dutiful father. "It's back to reality" he said, as he cradled his

baby daughter Georgia. "There have been a few times when I thought I was not going to see this through. But here I am. I'm glad that Tracey made me go back to Boston. Would I do something like this again? Never. Anyway, the wife wouldn't let me."

Angus McPhie, an optician from Devon, hung over the rail on *Heath Insured II*. "It's been a kaleidoscope of emotional experiences" he said. "Elation, dejection. Adrenaline, frustration. I've been absolutely pissed off, and wanted to punch the skipper on the nose. I've been at the helm in sixty knots, going through seas that will live with me for the rest of my life. Its rather like climbing Everest. Once you get to the top you realize you've achieved a great goal. You sit back and reflect. I'm glad to be alive, glad to be back with my family." Julia Bishop, on sixth-placed *Global Teamwork*, found herself pondering the lifelong lessons of self-reliance. "I've been exhausted, terrified" she said. "I've sobbed with pain, fatigue and frustration, yet somehow, from somewhere, I've found courage, resilience and strength I didn't know I possessed. That's the thing about the Challenge. You cope because there's no choice. The knowledge that I've always got that little bit extra to give will stay with me forever."

James Hatfield, skipper of the first fully disabled crew to sail around the world, had given as much of himself as humanly possible. He seemed distant, preoccupied, when he steered *Time & Tide* into Ocean Village just after breakfast the following morning. He was soaked by a fine rain and swamped by self-important local television reporters, who bellowed questions of the utmost inanity. The price of fulfilling his destiny had been onerous. He had lost friends, gained enemies, and hated the stigma of being last. The compensatory respect of those who put his achievement into the proper perspective would take time to register. "What can I say?" he pleaded. "I was always going to bring these guys back. It was tough, but they're used to

FAR LEFT: THE RACE IS WON, AN EXPERIENCE TO BE SHARED.

LEFT: WELCOME HOME DAD. FAMILY REUNION AT 4AM.

BELOW LEFT: A PRIVATE MOMENT IN A PUBLIC PLACE.

RIGHT: *GLOBAL TEAMWORK* GET THEIR CHAMPAGNE ON BOARD.

BELOW: PARTY BALLOONS GREET THE CREW ON *3COM*.

adversity. We've all scaled a huge learning curve. You realize you are not running a popularity contest out there, but we've shown the disabled community just what can be done." He was distracted by the sight of his mother in the crowd. Close to tears, he extended his arm towards her. "It's great to be back" he continued. "What a welcome. Unreal. The best."

Families were the lightning conductors of the BT Global Challenge. There was no more poignant sight, that morning, than IRA bomb victim Paul Burns. His three children, Ben, Georgina and John, clung desperately to him, as if they feared he was no more than a hologram. He was one of the heroes of the race, a man who suffered pain of unthinkable intensity on a daily basis. He deserved better than the indignity of having his marriage problems dissected in the Sunday papers, yet somehow remained philosophical. "It was worth it" he said. "It was the hardest thing I have ever done, and it has given me this amazing sense of relief and achievement. I've lived with tension for ten months, and maybe now I'll be able to take a big deep breath." The tears were there, though. They welled up in his eyes when someone asked him to outline the best thing about being home. "I don't need to say, do I?" he spluttered, drawing his children close to his chest.

LEFT: A WARM EARLY MORNING WELCOME FOR *TIME & TIDE*.

BELOW LEFT: THE OTHER CREWS AND THE PUBLIC WAITING IN OCEAN VILLAGE PROVIDE A RAPTUROUS RECEPTION AS *TIME & TIDE* DOCKS.

RIGHT: SIMPLY THE BEST. THE FIRST FULLY DISABLED CREW TO SAIL AROUND THE WORLD.

BELOW RIGHT: *TIME & TIDE* SKIPPER JAMES HATFIELD IS WELCOMED HOME.

As the crews dispersed, to face an uncertain future, Golding announced his plans with customary precision. Sorensen had sanctioned a new two-year Group 4 project, spanning both the Around Alone and the Vendee Globe solo circumnavigations. Merfyn Owen, the best of the Munificent Seven skippers, agreed to act as his campaign manager. The Fun Boy Three, Walker, Hindley and Lodge, had embellished their reputations, but others were deemed to have been relatively unsuccessful. Blyth, who had chosen from eighty-six potential skippers, recognized a lack of competitiveness and cohesive leadership skills in some of the also-rans. He acknowledged "being a skipper is a complex role" but had evidently resolved to act on hard lessons. He promised: "I'll be looking for different qualities of leadership and management on the next race. It will be more demanding, more competitive."

This begged the question whether Blyth would have met his own criteria. "I'm slow to praise and quick to criticize" he admitted with a wide smile. "I'm aware it's a bad trait. But, fortunately, I'm too old to go. So we'll never know the answer to that question." BT have an option on title sponsorship of the next Global Challenge, in the year 2000. It will feature a new fleet of between fifteen and twenty yachts, and only twenty crew places remain, for volunteers aged between twenty-five and thirty. Clearly, Blyth's surrogate family is destined to grow and grow. Typically, he was tickled by the symmetry of my first daughter, Lydia Joy, being born ten days after the race. "Aha" he said. "A crew volunteer for the Challenge in the year 2020. See you in the Guinness Bar."

Race Results and Crew Lists

FINAL STANDINGS

1ST ~ GROUP 4 SECURITAS

2ND ~ TOSHIBA WAVE WARRIOR

3RD ~ SAVE THE CHILDREN

4TH ~ MOTOROLA

5TH ~ COMMERCIAL UNION

6TH ~ GLOBAL TEAMWORK

7TH ~ NUCLEAR ELECTRIC

8TH ~ OCEAN ROVER

9TH ~ 3COM

10TH ~ PAUSE TO REMEMBER

11TH ~ COURTAULDS INTERNATIONAL

12TH ~ HEATH INSURED II

13TH ~ CONCERT

14TH ~ TIME & TIDE

LEFT: THE TRIUMPHANT *GROUP 4* CREW BREAK OPEN THE BUBBLY FOLLOWING THE TROPHY AWARDS FOR WINNING BOTH ANOTHER COURTAULDS TROPHY AS LEG WINNERS AND, MORE IMPORTANTLY, HAVING TAKEN THE OVERALL TITLE AS WINNERS OF THE BT GLOBAL CHALLENGE; SKIPPER MIKE GOLDING IS HOLDING THE LATTER ALOFT (FAR RIGHT).

Race Results

Leg One: Southampton to Rio de Janeiro

5,000 miles

Yacht	Time	Overall Time	Overall Position
Group 4	26 days 03 hours 47 mins 15 secs		
Toshiba Wave Warrior	26 days 05 hours 56 mins 11 secs		
Concert	26 days 14 hours 52 mins 23 secs		
Save the Children	26 days 22 hours 05 mins 39 secs		
Commercial Union	27 days 06 hours 58 mins 49 secs		
3Com	27 days 09 hours 34 mins 38 secs		
Motorola	27 days 14 hours 30 mins 55 secs		
Heath Insured II	27 days 16 hours 32 mins 03 secs		
Ocean Rover	27 days 18 hours 29 mins 48 secs		
Nuclear Electric	27 days 20 hours 30 mins 15 secs		
Global Teamwork	28 days 19 hours 43 mins 23 secs		
Pause to Remember	29 days 10 hours 36 mins 10 secs		
Courtaulds International	29 days 21 hours 14 mins 58 secs		
Time & Tide	29 days 23 hours 40 mins 33 secs		

Leg Two: Rio de Janeiro to Wellington

6,600 miles

Yacht	Time	Overall Time	Overall Position
Group 4	39 days 07 hours 16 mins 30 secs	65 days 11 hours 03 mins 45 secs	1st
Save the Children	39 days 10 hours 08 mins 13 secs	66 days 08 hours 13 mins 52 secs	3rd
Motorola	39 days 21 hours 07 mins 08 secs	67 days 11 hours 38 mins 03 secs	4th
Toshiba Wave Warrior	39 days 21 hours 27 mins 23 secs	66 days 03 hours 23 mins 34 secs	2nd
Global Teamwork	40 days 15 hours 05 mins 24 secs	69 days 10 hours 48 mins 47 secs	7th
Commercial Union	40 days 15 hours 15 mins 32 secs	67 days 22 hours 14 mins 21 secs	5th
Pause to Remember	40 days 20 hours 23 mins 30 secs	70 days 06 hours 59 mins 40 secs	10th
Nuclear Electric	41 days 03 hours 55 mins 37 secs	69 days 00 hours 25 mins 52 secs	6th
Ocean Rover	41 days 23 hours 05 mins 12 secs	69 days 17 hours 35 mins 00 secs	9th
Time & Tide	42 days 06 hours 42 mins 18 secs	72 days 06 hours 22 mins 51 secs	12th
3Com	42 days 07 hours 42 mins 43 secs	69 days 17 hours 17 mins 21 secs	8th
Courtaulds International	42 days 11 hours 54 mins 56 secs	72 days 09 hours 09 mins 54 secs	13th
Heath Insured II	43 days 23 hours 29 mins 06 secs	71 days 16 hours 01 mins 09 secs	11th
Concert	50 days 13 hours 48 mins 00 secs	77 days 04 hours 40 mins 23 secs	14th

Motorola (-8h 59m), 3Com (-5h 4m), Courtaulds International (-1h 55m) and Time & Tide (-6h 34m) were all given redress for rendering assistance.
Nuclear Electric was given a penalty (+5mins) incurred in Leg One.
Concert did not finish and received a finish time equal to Heath Insured II plus 15%.

Leg Three: Wellington to Sydney

1,230 miles

Yacht	Time	Overall Time	Overall Position
Save the Children	7 days 07 hours 32 mins 58 secs	73 days 15 hours 46 mins 50 secs	3rd
Group 4	7 days 09 hours 50 mins 44 secs	72 days 20 hours 54 mins 29 secs	1st
Courtaulds International	7 days 10 hours 51 mins 45 secs	79 days 20 hours 01 mins 39 secs	13th
Global Teamwork	7 days 11 hours 05 mins 03 secs	76 days 21 hours 53 mins 50 secs	7th
Pause to Remember	7 days 11 hours 17 mins 41 secs	77 days 18 hours 17 mins 21 secs	10th
Concert	7 days 11 hours 18 mins 32 secs	84 days 15 hours 58 mins 55 secs	14th
3Com	7 days 11 hours 19 mins 05 secs	77 days 04 hours 36 mins 26 secs	8th
Nuclear Electric	7 days 11 hours 33 mins 47 secs	76 days 12 hours 01 mins 26 secs	6th
Ocean Rover	7 days 11 hours 35 mins 34 secs	77 days 05 hours 08 mins 47 secs	9th
Toshiba Wave Warrior	7 days 11 hours 39 mins 30 secs	73 days 15 hours 03 mins 04 secs	2nd
Motorola	7 days 11 hours 41 mins 44 secs	74 days 23 hours 19 mins 47 secs	4th
Heath Insured II	7 days 12 hours 01 mins 01 secs	79 days 04 hours 02 mins 10 secs	11th
Commercial Union	7 days 12 hours 55 mins 11 secs	75 days 11 hours 09 mins 32 secs	5th
Time & Tide	7 days 13 hours 13 mins 48 secs	79 days 19 hours 36 mins 39 secs	12th

LEG FOUR: SYDNEY TO CAPE TOWN

6,200 miles

YACHT	TIME	OVERALL TIME	OVERALL POSITION
Group 4	37 days 23 hours 05 mins 05 secs	110 days 19 hours 59 mins 34 secs	1st
Concert	37 days 23 hours 25 mins 26 secs	122 days 15 hours 24 mins 21 secs	14th
Toshiba Wave Warrior	38 days 03 hours 11 mins 30 secs	111 days 18 hours 14 mins 34 secs	2nd
Commercial Union	38 days 18 hours 49 mins 23 secs	114 days 05 hours 58 mins 55 secs	5th
Motorola	39 days 03 hours 25 mins 27 secs	114 days 02 hours 45 mins 14 secs	4th
Save the Children	39 days 07 hours 23 mins 39 secs	112 days 23 hours 10 mins 29 secs	3rd
3Com	39 days 13 hours 43 mins 30 secs	116 days 18 hours 19 mins 56 secs	7th
Global Teamwork	39 days 14 hours 18 mins 51 secs	116 days 12 hours 12 mins 41 secs	6th
Ocean Rover	40 days 05 hours 15 mins 43 secs	117 days 10 hours 24 mins 30 secs	8th
Time & Tide	40 days 19 hours 37 mins 29 secs	120 days 15 hours 14 mins 08 secs	12th
Nuclear Electric	41 days 05 hours 37 mins 24 secs	117 days 17 hours 38 mins 50 secs	9th
Courtaulds International	41 days 09 hours 13 mins 30 secs	121 days 05 hours 15 mins 09 secs	13th
Pause to Remember	41 days 10 hours 03 mins 33 secs	119 days 04 hours 20 mins 54 secs	10th
Heath Insured II	41 days 10 hours 25 mins 48 secs	120 days 14 hours 27 mins 58 secs	11th

LEG FIVE: CAPE TOWN TO BOSTON

7,000 miles

YACHT	TIME	OVERALL TIME	OVERALL POSITION
Group 4	34 days 01 hours 48 mins 46 secs	144 days 21 hours 48 mins 20 secs	1st
Motorola	34 days 18 hours 12 mins 16 secs	148 days 20 hours 57 mins 30 secs	3rd
Toshiba Wave Warrior	35 days 07 hours 50 mins 14 secs	147 days 02 hours 04 mins 48 secs	2nd
Courtaulds International	35 days 12 hours 31 mins 05 secs	156 days 17 hours 46 mins 14 secs	11th
Concert	35 days 19 hours 34 mins 27 secs	158 days 10 hours 58 mins 48 secs	13th
Save the Children	36 days 00 hours 37 mins 54 secs	148 days 23 hours 48 mins 23 secs	4th
Commercial Union	36 days 04 hours 58 mins 38 secs	150 days 10 hours 57 mins 33 secs	5th
Nuclear Electric	36 days 07 hours 08 mins 59 secs	154 days 00 hours 47 mins 49 secs	7th
Global Teamwork	36 days 07 hours 15 mins 58 secs	152 days 19 hours 28 mins 39 secs	6th
Pause to Remember	36 days 13 hours 07 mins 07 secs	155 days 17 hours 28 mins 01 secs	10th
Heath Insured II	36 days 17 hours 59 mins 43 secs	157 days 08 hours 27 mins 41 secs	12th
Ocean Rover	36 days 23 hours 57 mins 35 secs	154 days 10 hours 22 mins 05 secs	9th
3Com	37 days 15 hours 57 mins 39 secs	154 days 10 hours 17 mins 35 secs	8th
Time & Tide	38 days 15 hours 50 mins 58 secs	159 days 07 hours 05 mins 06 secs	14th

Nuclear Electric (-1h 20m) and Heath Insured II (-30m) were both given redress for rendering assistance.
Save the Children (+3h 5m) and Time & Tide (+4h) were each given a penalty.

LEG SIX: BOSTON TO SOUTHAMPTON

3,000 miles

YACHT	TIME	OVERALL TIME	OVERALL POSITION
Group 4	16 days 07 hours 36 mins 58 secs	161 days 05 hours 25 mins 18 secs	1st
Toshiba Wave Warrior	16 days 09 hours 09 mins 46 secs	163 days 11 hours 14 mins 34 secs	2nd
Concert	16 days 10 hours 37 mins 41 secs	174 days 21 hours 36 mins 29 secs	13th
Save the Children	16 days 21 hours 02 mins 23 secs	165 days 20 hours 50 mins 46 secs	3rd
Commercial Union	16 days 21 hours 03 mins 59 secs	167 days 08 hours 01 mins 32 secs	5th
Nuclear Electric	17 days 00 hours 41 mins 21 secs	171 days 01 hours 29 mins 10 secs	7th
Global Teamwork	17 days 00 hours 59 mins 17 secs	169 days 20 hours 27 mins 56 secs	6th
Ocean Rover	17 days 01 hours 24 mins 29 secs	171 days 11 hours 46 mins 34 secs	8th
Heath Insured II	17 days 01 hours 36 mins 06 secs	174 days 10 hours 03 mins 47 secs	12th
3Com	17 days 01 hours 39 mins 55 secs	171 days 11 hours 57 mins 30 secs	9th
Courtaulds International	17 days 01 hours 39 mins 58 secs	173 days 19 hours 26 mins 12 secs	11th
Motorola	17 days 01 hours 43 mins 24 secs	165 days 22 hours 40 mins 54 secs	4th
Pause to Remember	17 days 01 hours 45 mins 27 secs	172 days 19 hours 13 mins 28 secs	10th
Time & Tide	17 days 11 hours 04 mins 49 secs	176 days 18 hours 09 mins 55 secs	14th

Time & Tide (-4h) was given redress on appeal.

Crew Lists

GROUP 4 SECURITAS

SKIPPER: MIKE GOLDING
Total crew used: 21

NAME	LEGS SAILED
Bacon, Andrea	Full Race
Banks, David	6th
Casely, Glenn	Full Race
Gibson, Grahame	Full Race
Girling, Andrew	Full Race
Hall, Martin	Full Race
Holliday, Chris	1st & 2nd
Jeffery, Tim*	3rd
Jones, David	4th
Malmberg, Loek	3rd
Neville, Adrian	5th
Pope, Andrew	Full Race
Robson, Timon	Full Race
Rollo, Nigel	5th
Shuff, Bill	Full Race
Sizer, Alex	Full Race
Smedley, Chris	6th
Tristram, Amanda	Full Race
Valentine, Kerry	1st
Ward, Jack	Full Race
Winfield, Grant	2nd & 4th

* Tim Jeffery also sailed on Courtaulds International for Legs Two and Six

TOSHIBA WAVE WARRIOR

SKIPPER: SIMON WALKER
Total crew used: 23

NAME	LEGS SAILED
Bell, Guy	1st, 2nd, 3rd & 6th
Briggs, Stewart	Full Race
Buerk, Michael	3rd
Crick, Judith	2nd
Dawson, Jo	Full Race
Day, Holly	3rd
Earle, Mark	Full Race
Edwards, Haydon	4th
Fernandez, Andrew	1st, 2nd, 3rd, 5th & 6th
Gaskin, Chris	1st & 4th
Goldie, Jack	6th
Heming, Diana	5th
Hodges, Justin	4th
Hutt, Mike	1st
Kotze, Kobus	Full Race
Morris, Angela	2nd, 4th & 5th
Pearson, Ben	Full Race

NAME	LEGS SAILED
Peek, Roger	6th
Scott, Ciara	Full Race
Sears, Alan	Full Race
Ward, Geoff	Full Race
Watson, Joanne	Full Race
Watson, Keith	5th

SAVE THE CHILDREN

SKIPPER: ANDY HINDLEY
Total crew used: 29

NAME	LEGS SAILED
Allard, Tim	2nd
Bishop, Peter	6th
Bolger, Reg	5th
Chalk, Simon	2nd
Drayner, Ian	1st
Fairhurst, Alison	5th
Garside, Diana	Full Race
Hodgson, Warren	3rd
Hoyle, Suzanne	5th
Hughes, Sarah	2nd
Johnson, Ian	6th
Johnson, Kevin	Full Race
Jones, Robin	1st
Kinast, Kurt	1st & 2nd
Kruse, Bryan	4th
Lindon, Rosemary	1st
Lockwood, Michael	Full Race
Prior, Tim	4th
Sherwood, Paul	Full Race
Stevens, Rod	Full Race
Stubbs, Robert	Full Race
Taylor, Jonathan	Full Race
Thatcher, Sue	3rd, 4th, 5th & 6th
Vaulbert de Chantilly, Elizabeth	3rd
Waslidge, Anne	4th
White, Phillip	Full Race
White, Richard	3rd
Wolter, Ian	Full Race
Yates, John	6th

MOTOROLA

SKIPPER: MARK LODGE
Total crew used: 33

NAME	LEGS SAILED
Aitchison, John	1st, 2nd & 3rd
Baptist, Mark	Full Race
Bell, Valerie	1st & 2nd

NAME	LEGS SAILED
Breen, Tim	1st
Broderick, Michael	2nd
Burge, Christine	Full Race
Burns, Alastair	Full Race
Calvin, Michael	3rd
Challis, Ben	3rd
Chatwin, Robert	Full Race
Crozier, John	Full Race
Dobbin, John	6th
Fleming, Lucy	5th
Ford, Kate*	4th
Gibbons, David	2nd
Gooding, Stephen	Full Race
Harrison, Dale	4th & 6th
Keighley, Kester	4th & 6th
Lister, David	5th
Miles, Peter	Full Race
Moore, Ann	5th
Netto, Ben	4th
Nightingale, Darren	5th
Oliver, Alan	4th
Park, Suzanne	1st
Pollard, Richard	1st
Ripper, Ligia	Full Race
Roe, Willo	6th
Rose, David	2nd
Smyth, Kevin	3rd
Titford, Douglas	6th
Wentzel, Adrian	5th
Wyre, Steve	3rd

* Kate Ford also sailed on Courtaulds International for Leg Three

COMMERCIAL UNION ASSURANCE

SKIPPER: RICHARD MERRIWEATHER
Total crew used: 21

NAME	LEGS SAILED
Allpress, Claire	Full Race
Auger, Nick	Full Race
Bean, Bransom	Full Race
Blowers, Sean	1st & 2nd
Bourke, Lorna	6th
Burrows, Tim	Full Race
Corner, Trevor	Full Race
Desmond, Jim	4th
Douglas, Margot	Full Race
Eatough, Neil	Full Race
Hake, Joanne	5th
Hampson, Ian	Full Race
Harper, Vicky	1st
Hood, Stewart	3rd
Hultgren, Lars	Full Race
Klaasen-Bos, Madelene	2nd
Moran, Eileen	Full Race
Porter, Glenda	6th
Reynolds, Ian	3rd
Shanks, David	Full Race
Thomas, Alan	4th & 5th

GLOBAL TEAMWORK

SKIPPER: MERFYN OWEN
Total crew used: 25

NAME	LEGS SAILED
Adams, Elaine	Full Race
Arnold, Roger	1st, 3rd, 5th & 6th
Atkinson, Scott	4th
Bishop, Julia	Full race
Craig, Peter	Full race
Cunningham, Gordon	2nd
Goode, Angela	5th
Harrison, Kit	Full race
Hughes, Glyn	Full race
Jenkins, Rhian*	Full race
Kay, Michael	4th
Lane, Anthony	1st
Lear, Mary	6th
Longden, Andrew	1st
Manzoni, James	4th
Poulsom, Vivienne	3rd
Rudge, Alan•	3rd
Rudge, Peter	2nd
Schreurs, Lucas	Full race
Scott, John	Full race
Stephens, Will	Full race
Sutton, Stuart	2nd
Taylor, Roger	Full race
Walker, Graham	6th
Wharton, Brian	5th

* Counted as Full Race despite missing part through medical evacuation
• Alan Rudge also sailed on Concert for Leg Six

NUCLEAR ELECTRIC

SKIPPER: RICHARD TUDOR
Total crew used: 25

NAME	LEGS SAILED
Baker, Mark	3rd
Beever, Richard	6th
Bentley, Helen	Full Race
Brown, David	1st
Calvin, Peter	Full Race
Clarke, Duncan	2nd, 3rd, 4th, 5th & 6th
Day, Derek	1st
Egan, Paul	1st
Johnstone, Mark	Full Race
Lyon, Malcolm	2nd
McGuire, Vinn	4th
Mann, Tony	Full Race
Montague, Simon	Full Race
Murray, Fiona	1st
Nash, Jon	2nd
Palmer, Lesley	3rd
Park, Dorothy	2nd, 3rd, 4th, 5th & 6th

NAME	LEGS SAILED
Parry-Jones, Gwen	5th
Rodebjer, Håkan	Full Race
Scott, Ian	5th
Walters, Jocelyn	Full Race
Wardle, Simon	Full Race
Wakins, David	6th
Wattling, Alan	4th
Williams, John	Full Race

OCEAN ROVER

SKIPPER: PAUL BENNETT
Total crew used: 24

NAME	LEGS SAILED
Brighton, Richard	6th
Bruce, Robert	Full Race
Capstick, James	Full Race
Clifton, Paul	4th
Cotterill, Wendy	5th
Davies, Collette	1st
Fell, Simon	2nd
Fogerty, Hugh	Full Race
Guy, Lyn	Full Race
Hirsh, Jon	Full Race
Hollingsworth, Anthony	Full Race
Islef, Lennert	2nd
Jackson, Randal	4th
Kennedy, David	Full Race
HRH Prince Michael of Kent	3rd
Lacey, Jim	4th
Simmons, Maureen	Full Race
Soanes, Julian	1st
Stephens, Paul	1st, 2nd, 3rd, 5th & 6th
Stevens, Rachel	5th
Thornton, William	Full Race
Walker, Malcolm	6th
Walters, Humphrey	Full Race
Whiting, Allan	3rd

3COM

SKIPPER: DAVID TOMLINSON
Total crew used: 28

NAME	LEGS SAILED
Akerman, Piers	3rd
Belbin, David	4th
Bibby, Ian	1st, 2nd, 3rd, 5th & 6th
Carter, Andrea	1st & 2nd
Chaplin, Kate	Full Race
Constable, Alex	3rd
Corfield, Jane	Full Race
Donkin, Richard	2nd
Falle, Philippe	Full Race
Gent, Paul	4th
Griffiths, Alan	5th
McGarrick, Peter	1st

Measures, Kathryn	3rd, 4th, 5th & 6th
O'Connell, Kieron	Full Race
Pilkington, Carol	6th
Pizarro, Christian	6th
Pryce, David	4th
Reid, Mary	5th
Sadler, Will	Full Race
Shah, Rohit	1st
Sketch, Nikki	4th
St John Martin, Paul	5th
Thornley, Malcolm	Full Race
Townsend, Johnathon	Full Race
Walker, Gerrard	1st, 2nd & 6th
Ward, Mark	Full Race
Windsor, Jane	3rd
Williamson, Stuart	2nd

PAUSE TO REMEMBER

SKIPPER: TOM O'CONNOR
Total crew used: 23

NAME	LEGS SAILED
Barham, Jim	6th
Barrett, Frank	5th
Claggs, Susan	5th
Davis, Julian	Full Race
Driver, Nick	4th
Goddard, Ronald	Full Race
Grenville, Andrew	2nd
Hall, Anna	2nd
Hamilton, Lesley	4th
Haynes, Rebecca	Full Race
Humphries, Janet	Full Race
Kay, Bruce	Full Race
Maton, Genevieve	1st
O'Flynn, Caspar	Full Race
Philp, Graham	Full Race
Price, Christopher	Full Race
Pritchard, Henry	Full Race
Reeves, Matthew	Full Race
Seifert, Rainer	Full Race
Swingewood, John	3rd
Tipper, Janet	3rd
Treagust, Angela	1st
Williams, Clive	6th

COURTAULDS INTERNATIONAL

SKIPPER: BORIS WEBBER
Total crew used: 32

NAME	LEGS SAILED
Alson, Laurent	5th
Bell, Craig	4th & 5th
Bray, Melissa	2nd
Buller, Jackie	6th
Callahan, Steven	5th

Name	Leg Sailed
Chatwin, Anthony	1st, 2nd, 4th, 5th & 6th
Collett, Paul	1st, 2nd, 3rd, 4th & 6th
Coomer, Lytton	5th
Dahlberg, Claes	3rd
Ford, Kate*	3rd
Gaisford, Richard	6th
Goulder, Susan	Full Race
Greaves, David	1st, 2nd & 3rd
Jameson, Thomas	2nd
Jeffery, Tim•	2nd & 6th
Leadbeater, Michael	Full Race
Letty, Rebecca	1st
Masters, Alison	3rd
Mattson, Lina	1st
Metcalf, Howard	1st & 2nd
Moss, Colin	Full Race
O'Ryan, David	Full Race
Redman, Patricia	1st & 6th
Roberson, John	4th
Rowe, Richard	Full Race
Saint-Jour, Pierre	5th
Timmis, Dianne	4th, 5th & 6th
Tinson, Carl	Full Race
Tomlinson, Rick	3rd
Watson, Stewart	4th
Wheatley, Keith	3rd
White, Tom	4th

* Kate Ford also sailed on Motorola for Leg Four
• Tim Jeffery also sailed on Group 4 Securitas for Leg Three

HEATH INSURED II

SKIPPER: ADRIAN DONOVAN
Total crew used: 22

Name	Leg Sailed
Babcock, Michael	Full Race
Betts, Nigel	Full Race
Bracher, David	Full Race
Carter, Martin	4th
Delbridge, Peter	1st

Name	Leg Sailed
Gillespie, Julia	Full Race
Grover, Simon	5th & 6th
Heddon, Paula	1st
Jardine, Sue	1st
Justsum, Alan	3rd
McPhie, Angus	Full Race
Neate, David	4th & 5th
Orrock, Jason	2nd
Pilkington, Andrew*	Full Race
Rowen, Liz	2nd, 3rd, 4th, 5th & 6th
Shiels, Paul	3rd
Shufflebottom, John	Full Race
Stewart, Sally	Full Race
Thomas, Howard	2nd & 6th
Van der Hoff, John	Full Race
Wedel, Anders	4th
Whaley, Adrian	1st, 2nd, 3rd, 5th & 6th

* Counted as Full Race despite missing part through medical evacuation

CONCERT

SKIPPER: CHRIS TIBBS
Total crew used: 21

Name	Legs Sailed
Angell, Richard	1st, 2nd, 3rd, 5th & 6th
Beaumont, Brian	Full Race
Brice, Sarah	Full Race
Bulmer, Beverley	6th
Cooper, John	Full Race
Duncan, Lucy	Full Race
Ede, Lisa	5th
Fletcher, Matthew	Full Race
Harrison, Edward	Full Race
Haynes, Robin	1st
Keating, John	Full Race
Kennard, Naomi	Full Race
McElligott, John	5th
McMahon, Corey	4th
Pask, Stuart	Full Race

Name	Leg Sailed
Pilkington, Adrian	1st, 2nd, 3rd & 4th
Pratt, Lucy	3rd
Raea, Steve	2nd
Rudge, Alan*	6th
Wakeling, Philip	Full Race
Willdig, Keith	4th

* Alan Rudge also sailed on Global Teamwork for Leg Three

TIME & TIDE

SKIPPER: JAMES HATFIELD
Total crew used: 27

Name	Leg Sailed
Anderson, John	2nd
Austin, Mike	2nd & 3rd
Boreham, Stuart	1st, 5th & 6th
Bowden, Lesley	Full Race
Burns, Paul	Full Race
Davies, Carolyn	Full Race
Dutton, Clive	4th
Gledhill, Anthony	3rd
Hammond, Greg	5th
Hebblethwaite, Paul	Full Race
Hodder, David	1st
Horton Fawkes, Richard	1st
Latter, Steven	4th
McKeag, Malcolm	3rd
Morphew, Geoff	3rd
Needs, Simon	6th
Ogg, Chris	Full Race
Rayner, Grahme	4th, 5th & 6th
Rich, John	1st & 2nd
Sear, Carol	2nd, 3rd, 4th, 5th & 6th
Smith, Nigel	Full Race
Spence, John	5th
Tabor, Colin	6th
Tait, David	Full Race
Tring, Liz	1st, 2nd & 3rd
West, Brendan	2nd, 5th & 6th
Williams, Greg	1st

Acknowledgments and Picture Credits

ACKNOWLEDGMENTS
The publisher, author and photographer would like to thank the following individuals and organizations without whose assistance the book would not have been possible: Nigel Pyke, Paul Stringer and Phil London at British Telecommunications plc; Adrian Rayson and staff at the BT Global Challenge Race Office; the staff at The Challenge Business Limited for their help with information and crew lists; Martin Smithers and staff at the Royal Ocean Racing Club for their assistance with the race results information; and Debbie Cartwright, Judy Hill and Tony Rayner at the BBC. A special thank you ought also to go to Martin, Fiona, Ian and Stuart of The Challenge Business Limited for the rewarding cruise in the Solent.

BT and the Piper logo are trademarks of British Telecommunications plc. Concert is a trademark of Concert Communications Company.

PICTURE CREDITS
All the images reproduced in the book were supplied by Mark Pepper Photography (MPP). Unless credited otherwise below, all the images were taken by Mark Pepper and/or MPP and are copyright of British Telecommunications plc. A number of the on board pictures were taken by crew; MPP, BT and the publisher would like to extend their thanks to these crew volunteers. Pictures are listed below by page and position.

Page 1: Philippe Falle; **2–3:** Jon Nash/PPL, ref JNA 29015221M; **4–5:** Motorola crew/MPP; **6–7:** Martin Hayhow/MPP; **8:** British Steel/PPL Limited, ref BST 29014576M; **10:** DML Devonport, ref 90028A-6; **11:** (top) Colin Beere/BT, (bottom) Eric North; **12:** DML Devonport, ref 95562A-3; **36:** (bottom) Langdon/MPP; **40:** Hugh Routledge/MPP; **42–43:** 3Com, Group 4, Commercial Union, Save the Children, Global Teamwork and Pause to Remember crews/MPP; **44:** (bottom) Richard Langdon/MPP; **46:** (bottom) Time & Tide crew/MPP; **48:** (top) Stephen Munday/Allsport; **56:** (bottom) Hood Sailmakers Ltd via Tracie Currie; **57:** (top) Global Teamwork crew MPP; **59:** Jon Nash; **60–61:** Jon Nash/PPL, ref JNA 29014673M; **62:** (both) Save the Children crew/MPP; **64–65:** (all) Concert crew/MPP; **66:** (top) Save the Children crew/MPP, (bottom) Global Teamwork crew/MPP; **67:** (left, top and bottom) Motorola crew/MPP, (right) Concert crew/MPP; **69:** (top left) Global Teamwork crew/MPP, (bottom left) Jon Nash, (top right) Concert crew/MPP; **76:** Concert crew/MPP; **82–83:** Rick Tomlinson, ref BTC96C 2221; **86–87:** Rick Tomlinson, ref BTC96C 0472; **88:** (top) Robert Bruce/Allsport; **92–93:** Jon Nash/PPL; **96:** (top) Chris Kapetanellis/MPP; **98–99:** Mike Cooper/Allsport; **100:** (bottom) Rick Tomlinson, ref BTC96C0433; **101:** (top) Toshiba Wave Warrior crew/MPP, (bottom) Global Teamwork crew/MPP; **102–103:** (both) Global Teamwork crew/MPP; **104:** Courtaulds International crew/MPP; **105:** Boris Webber/MPP; **106–107:** Save the Children crew/MPP; **108:** (top) Group 4 crew/MPP, (bottom) Time & Tide crew/MPP; **109:** (top) Time & Tide crew/MPP, (bottom) Save the Children crew/MPP; **110:** (both) Pause to Remember crew/MPP; **115:** (bottom) Clive Mason/Allsport; **119:** (top) Stephen Munday/Allsport; **122–123:** Stephen Munday/Allsport; **124:** (top) Pause to Remember crew/MPP, (bottom) Courtaulds International crew/MPP; **125:** (left) Save the Children crew/MPP, (right) Time & Tide crew/MPP; **126:** (top) Group4 crew/MPP; **127:** (top) Concert crew/MPP, (bottom) Toshiba Wave Warrior crew/MPP; **128–129:** Motorola, Group 4, Commercial Union, Save the Children, Global Teamwork and Toshiba Wave Warrior crews/MPP; **132:** (top) Peter McGowan/MPP; **136:** (top) © Mark Pepper; **137:** Peter McGowan/MPP; **140–141:** Peter McGowan/MPP; **142–143:** (all) Toshiba Wave Warrior crew/MPP; **144:** Global Teamwork crew/MPP; **145:** (both) Commercial Union crew/MPP; **146:** (sequence of three) Rick Tomlinson; **148–149:** (all) Richard Langdon/MPP; **151:** (bottom) Richard Langdon/MPP; **159:** (Boris Webber) Rick Tomlinson, ref BTC96C0182.

South
DEPAR
WAYPOINT MARK
Leg Six : 3000 miles
Gulf Stream
Boston
DEPART 29 June 1997
ATLANTIC OCEAN
Leg Five : 7000 miles
Leg One : 5000 miles
TROPIC OF CANCER
NORTH EAST TRADES
DOLDRUMS
EQUATOR
South Equitorial Curren
SOUTH EAST TRADE
Rio de Janeiro
DEPART 20 November 1996
TROPIC OF CAPRICORN
Brazil Current
PACIFIC OCEAN
Cape Horn
Leg Two : 6600 miles
WAYPOINT MARK
ROARING FORTIES
ROA